To the 127th Military Police Company,
and all those who have served.

Collins is an imprint of HarperCollins Publishers.
HarperTeen is an imprint of HarperCollins Publishers.

Youngbloods quote page 118 based on the article "Buffalo Springfield"
by Paul Williams, *Crawdaddy!*, March 1967

Library of Congress Cataloging-in-Publication Data
Kohler, Dean Ellis.
 Rock 'n' roll soldier / by Dean Ellis Kohler ; with Susan VanHecke. — 1st ed.
  p. cm.
 ISBN 978-0-06-124255-7
 1. Vietnam War, 1961–1975—Personal narratives, American—Juvenile literature.
 2. Kohler, Dean Ellis—Juvenile literature. 3. United States. Army—Military police—
Biography—Juvenile literature. 4. Rock musicians—United States—Biography—
Juvenile literature. I. VanHecke, Susan. II. Title.
DS559.5.K625 2009   2008047702
959.704'3373092—dc22   CIP
[B]   AC

Typography by Matt Adamec
09 10 11 12 13 CG/RRDB 10 9 8 7 6 5 4 3 2 1

First Edition

ROCK 'N' ROLL SOLDIER
A Memoir

By Dean Ellis Kohler
with Susan VanHecke

Collins

HARPER TEEN
An Imprint of HarperCollinsPublishers

FOREWORD

In many ways, the Vietnam War and the present wars in the Middle East seem frighteningly similar. Both sprang from disputed, even dubious, origins. A precise definition of "the enemy" continues to be elusive. And opinions of both conflicts remain deeply divided.

During the Vietnam War, my musical partners David Crosby, Stephen Stills, Neil Young, and I spoke out passionately against the madness we saw taking place in Southeast Asia. Yet we just as vigorously supported the troops for the difficult job they'd been asked to perform. As we do now, we wished them the very best in their challenging mission and hoped for their safe return.

Since Vietnam, we've been approached by countless veterans who've thanked us for speaking our minds. More importantly, they've told us that it was music—our music, our friends' music—that helped them get through another day to survive for another night . . . and to get through another night to survive for another day.

As a young soldier in Vietnam, Dean Kohler learned firsthand about music's lifesaving power. With a few fellow GIs and some improvised equipment, he formed a fully functional, touring rock band in the midst of the war zone. What began simply as an order from his commanding officer ultimately became a lifeline for Dean and the band, as well as the thousands of combat-weary troops they played for.

Through the transcendent power of music, Dean created his own bit of order out of the chaos of the Vietnam War . . . to survive another day.

This is his remarkable story.

—Graham Nash

Author's Note

I first heard of the Vietnam War in 1963. I was sitting on our family-room floor, painting a plaster-of-Paris volcano for my tenth-grade science class. The TV news was on. I wasn't paying much attention—until they started showing pictures of people setting themselves on fire in a place called Vietnam. I couldn't look away.

It was horrifying and fascinating all at the same time. And it all seemed so weird, so distant. So nothing to do with me.

Many years later, I'd learn that the people were Buddhist monks protesting the regime of South Vietnamese president Ngo Dinh Diem. In 1954, when Vietnam won its independence from France, the region had been split in half. Communist leader Ho Chi Minh established his government in North Vietnam and Diem led non-Communist South Vietnam. By 1963, Diem was convinced that Buddhists in his country were assisting the Viet Cong, guerilla fighters believed to be aligned with North Vietnam, which wanted a reunified, Communist Vietnam. Though the majority of South Vietnamese were Buddhist, Diem brutally enforced anti-Buddhism laws.

Thanks in part to those horrific Buddhist protests, Diem was deposed and executed by members of his own military in early November 1963. It was three weeks before the assassination of U.S. president John F. Kennedy, who by 1961 had already established a U.S. presence in the area, sending equipment and advisers to help the South Vietnamese in their fight.

The struggle between North and South Vietnam, between Communist and non-Communist states, continued after the deaths of Diem and JFK. Not that I gave it much thought. I was busy with school, girls, cars, and my rock band, the Satellites.

In August 1964, the summer before my senior year in high school, the North Vietnamese military attacked U.S. Navy ships off the Vietnamese coast. Congress quickly passed the Gulf of Tonkin Resolution, giving President Lyndon B. Johnson authorization to use military force in Southeast Asia. American soldiers were ordered into the region by the thousands.

By the time I graduated, in 1965, I was definitely paying attention. The number of American troops in Vietnam had gone from around 3,000 in 1961 to 180,000 in 1965.

They'd eventually top 500,000 in 1968. Ugly pictures were just starting to come back from the front lines, news photos of villagers whose homes had been torched in search-and-destroy missions, fueling the first of what would be countless antiwar protests in the U.S. over the next few years.

Buddies I knew from high school were being drafted and sent to Vietnam nearly every month. They'd be going about their business, working at their jobs or getting ready to go off to college. And then—*poof*—they were just gone.

For some reason, I never really thought it could happen to me.

Then I got my draft notice.

I said good-bye to family and friends in March 1966 and boarded the train bound for basic training. It was the beginning of a journey that would take me to places I never could have fathomed, to see and do things I never could have imagined. With me for the life-altering ride were my brave friends in the Army's 127th MP Company.

Although I've taken a certain author's license in telling our story, the soldiers of the 127th and their lives and times were real. I've used actual names for most of the people in this book and pseudonyms for others. For clarity, I've also taken some liberties in the telling of our tale, particularly in reconstruction of dialogue and correspondence, creation of composite characters, and the precise sequence of events.

My intent, always, was to allow the truth of our experience to shine brightly.

1

WELCOME TO NAM

"There it is, man—Vietnam!"

"Better watch your ass, Charlie! Army's here and we takin' you suckers out!"

"No mercy, you sorry bastards!"

I wished they'd all just shut up. For the first time in the month it'd taken the USS *Upshur* to carry me and four thousand of my closest army pals across the Pacific, I couldn't breathe.

Come on, Kohler, inhale. Exhale.

Maybe it was the heat. Even though it was January, the air was so thick, so chest-stomping hot, it seemed to suck the breath right out of my lungs. My fatigues were dripping wet.

Like the rest, I kept a tight grip on my bulletless M14. No ammo; they didn't want us shooting each other, or ourselves, on the way over. The rifle felt like a two-ton barbell in my hands. *Man, what I wouldn't give for a breeze.* I leaned against the railing, my face to the sinking sun, and fought the urge to puke.

"Dean, you cool, man?" asked Jon Sugden, slouching next to me.

"Yeah," I lied. "I'm cool."

"Guess we're here," Sugden said, his face a blank behind his government-issue horn-rims.

Is he scared? I wondered but couldn't bring myself to ask. Definitely wouldn't be cool. *Are they all scared? Is that why they won't shut up?*

"Yeah," I mumbled. "Guess so."

My arms felt like rubber.

In the purple-red glow, I could just make out the shore and jungle and wrinkled mountains off in the distance. It looked like a vacation postcard.

So this was it—Nam. No turning back now. Something shifted in my stomach.

The bay looked like a giant bathtub full of toy boats. Carriers with jets poised for takeoff, red lights blinking. Battleships, their massive gun barrels silhouetted against the horizon. Small destroyers scattered about like gray bobbers.

Then, from out of nowhere, a bomber buzzed in over the beach. Above the jungle, flying low, set the palm trees swaying. Hugged the shoreline and started dropping his payload. Split second, and everything blew up behind him, giant balls of fire, as Technicolor red as the Saigon sunset. Beautiful. Terrifying. I couldn't look away. It swept over a few more times, laying great trails of flame and smoke behind it, then flew off. Just like a movie.

Only it was real.

By the next morning, January 7, 1967, we'd finally made it up the coast to Qui Nhon. A storm had moved in overnight, the wind so wild we could hear it whistling through the ship's passageways.

Captain Leadbetter mustered the four platoons of the 127th Military Police Company, all 177 of us, belowdecks. Didn't look like anybody'd slept—we were all bleary-eyed and jittery. No macho talk this morning.

"This is where we get off, soldiers," Captain barked as he paced in front of us. "Weather's too sloppy for the ship to dock, so we're moving to Plan B. Saddle up and fall in on the top deck, pronto."

"In the rain, sir?" somebody asked.

"That's right. We've got a bus to catch."

Within minutes we were struggling against the gale as we climbed in full pack-gear—seventy-pound duffels over one shoulder, rifles over the other—out onto the deck. Between the pelting rain and the spume of waves crashing against the ship, I could hardly make out what was in front of me. I squinted to keep the water out of my eyes.

"Line up and drop off!" Captain ordered above the

storm's roar. With a beefy arm he pointed to a cargo net flapping from the deck ten feet down the ship's hull. "Go! Now!"

Our near-year of training kicked in. One after another, the guys ahead of me scrambled down the dancing rope ladder and dropped into small metal boats—beach landing craft—waiting below. They looked like soggy green balls rolling out of a giant, gray gum-ball machine. Some jumped without a word. Others let out choked cries or kamikaze whoops.

My teeth clenched as I got closer to the side; my soaked pack cut into my shoulder. This was crazy. The net twisted in the storm. The boats pitched and lurched on an ocean that churned like some weird washing machine set on warp.

A blast of salt spray, and everything went blurry. I could just make out the kid in front of me grabbing the ladder and working his way down. As he let go, a huge wave tossed the troop boat forward. I watched, frozen, as the soldier disappeared into the raging sea.

"Man overboard!" screamed the sailor in the doorway as he flung orange flotation rings out into the crashing waves.

I couldn't move. Who was it? Most of us had been together since the six months of MP school back at Fort Gordon. We were a team, a family, almost. *Don't let him die, please don't let him die.*

A head finally popped up. Knutsen, the California surfer.

If anybody knew his way in the water, it was Knutsen. Struggling and gasping, still clutching his pack and rifle, he swam for a ring. The boat pulled up next to him, soldiers reaching through the spray to grab him. Just as they seemed to have him, another enormous wave slapped the landing craft sidelong, sending it careening toward the ship's steel hull, Knutsen in its path. An instant before he would have been crushed, the troops pulled Knutsen up and into the bow.

Then it was my turn.

"Jump, Kohler! Move it!" Captain roared.

My knees felt like jelly. I could hear the blood pounding in my ears.

Please, God. I sucked in my breath, willed my feet forward, and worked my way to the bottom of the net. I dangled for a second—*please, please*—then leaped, legs tucked, into the wind.

I landed with a sodden jolt on the metal floor, the force knocking my teeth together. Sanchez and Callahan cheered as they pulled me out of the way. Three more soldiers tumbled into the boat behind me. Water sloshed over and around all of us.

When the whole company was loaded, the four boats labored through the froth to shore. We clung to the sides and one another, then rolled out like turtles on our backs as the craft hit the beach. "Move! Move!" Captain and the lieutenants bellowed. No time to think, just go. We followed orders and slogged through the thick red mud, spitting out mouthfuls and shaking it out of our ears as we made our way to firmer ground.

My arms and legs kept pumping, but my mind was stuck on one terrifying thought: We were unarmed and exposed. Wide open. What if Charlie was waiting for us with gunfire or mortar rounds? We'd be toast, plain and simple. Sitting ducks. But what could we do? My skin prickled. There was no choice—we had to trust that Captain knew what he was doing.

Thankfully, he did. No enemy. Instead, there were big, brown buses circled by tough-looking soldiers who offered no help and seemed bored. It was obvious that, to them, we were just another load of stupid FNGs, Fucking New Guys.

"Looks like the limos are here." Mike Ioli panted in front of me. A few of the guys snickered halfheartedly as we waded through the mire that reeked of dead fish and raw sewage. All of us were coated with it.

Grateful to be out of the rain and the muck, we boarded the buses. I collapsed in a seat next to Wright.

"Hey, what's with the metal grates over the windows?" somebody behind us yelled to a stocky lifer type standing guard outside the bus.

"Keeps out the grenades," he grunted.

"Great," I muttered, and shifted uncomfortably in my seat. What kind of place was this?

Captain stood at the front of the bus as we took off through the rain. "Welcome to the city of Qui Nhon, the *Ree*-public of Vietnam, your home away from home for the next year," he hollered over the engine's chug. "You *will* stay safe and all in one piece here if you use common sense and remember your training. The enemy—Charlie, the Viet Cong, VC, whatever you want to call him—is sneaky. And Charlie doesn't play by the rules. Watch out for the snakes, the bugs, and the girls—you can't trust any of them. Keep alert, stay smart, and you'll get back home alive."

Home alive. That's all I wanted to hear. Man, my stomach hurt.

Home. I closed my eyes and thought about what they might be doing back home. Definitely not leaping from ships, crawling through mud, or providing target practice for the Viet Cong.

No, this morning at home had probably unrolled like every morning in Portsmouth, Virginia. Mom at the stove, as usual, cooking up breakfast. Eggs, bacon, and toast for Dad. French toast, my favorite, for Mary. Dad skimming the newspaper, slurping his black coffee. Mary upstairs, primping in the bathroom, until Mom called her down so she wouldn't be late for school.

When I was still around, Mom would send us all off with a perfumed hug after breakfast. Dad would carpool to his desk job at the city water department. I'd drop Mary off at Cradock High on my way to my job at the land surveyor's.

7

It was an okay gig, I guess, for someone like me, fresh out of high school. Pretty boring, though. I'd punch the clock, then count down the hours until quitting time and band practice at Uncle Roy's. We'd set up in his living room, learn some new songs, gear up for the next show. Or the big recording session. *Oh, right. That.*

If I weren't here, I would be cutting a record right now.

I gritted my teeth and opened my eyes. There wasn't much to look at through the grating, just watery green fields rolling by in the downpour. It looked peaceful, almost pretty. Like a place you might want to visit.

"Rice paddies," somebody said.

"They're everywhere," said another. "Must eat a lot of friggin' rice here."

"That's where Charlie likes to hide," said Lieutenant Vedlitz.

Nobody said much else.

Soon, the buses eased to a stop at the base of a tall mountain covered with shrub and bamboo. Air brakes hissed and the doors squeaked open onto a giant field of mud. On one end was a paddy, pimpled by raindrops; on the other, a cemetery, stone markers glistening like pawns on a chessboard.

"Under a mountain, now that's just great." Wright snorted. "VC won't even need a tube to nail us with a mortar. They can chuck 'em right off the side."

"Aw, that wouldn't be neighborly," I tried to joke.

But I knew he was probably right.

DODGE CITY

"**G**rab your gear and let's make camp before sundown!" Leadbetter barked. "Now get moving!"

As we stepped off the buses, a small fleet of deuce-and-a-halfs, the army's two-and-a-half-ton cargo trucks, rumbled up, loaded to the brim with crates and canvas.

We dropped our duffels and set to work in the rain, pulling supplies and equipment off the backs of the trucks. Our rifles were still useless and we all kept wary eyes on the mountain, the paddy, the graveyard.

Captain, his pipe clamped in the corner of his mouth, strode the muddy field with the lieutenants, supervising the operation. Some guys started stringing yards of concertina—double coils of razor wire stretched out like a spring—on our perimeter, and others began constructing front and back gates. I fell in with Ioli and Sugden and the rest of Three Squad, Third Platoon, setting up a GP

Medium—army general-purpose tent sleeps a full squad, a dozen soldiers.

"Just like old times," Ioli said to no one in particular as he unfolded the green canvas just as we'd done so often in training. "Feels good to be doing something normal."

I nodded and the knots in my stomach loosened just a little. I grabbed a length of ridge beam.

The rain had eased to a soft drizzle and the sky brightened from charcoal to steel. The heavy air still stank, and our boots were like ice skates on the slick mud.

I held the piece of beam as Sugden bolted it to another. His mud-caked face was expressionless as he worked the pliers.

"So what do you think, man?" I asked, fighting to keep my feet from sliding out from under me.

He pushed his mud-spattered specs on his nose. "God's country," he said drily, and gave the bolt another twist. "Doing God's work."

As usual, Sugden's sarcasm got a chuckle out of me, even as my feet sank in the mud up to my ankles. We'd been pretty much inseparable since we'd met at Fort Gordon in Augusta—"Disgusta," as Sugden fondly called it—Georgia. We were both into music. Sug liked all the same stuff I did, the Ventures, Chet Atkins, Duane Eddy. On the ride over, I'd even taught him how to play a little bass on the bottom strings of a couple of guitars we'd borrowed from the ship's chaplain.

"Goddamn it!" Ioli, who had been folding up the tent walls to expose the metal plates for the ridge mast, lost his footing and landed face-first in the mud.

"Freakin' rain!" he spluttered as the rest of us grinned. "Freakin' mud all over the damn place!" He scooped the goop from his eyes and flung it to the ground, then wiped his muddy hands on his muddy shirt. He looked up to the sky. "Man, I wish I was back on the Jersey Shore. Drinking some cold brews, killing a pepperoni pie, and checking out the hot bikinis." He stood up and shook like a wet dog, bits of mud flying in every direction.

"Yeah, you'd be getting all sorts of action lookin' like that," Halloran drawled in his Alabama twang.

"I swear, you guys, we gotta be making camp on a cesspool or something," Ioli groused as he helped Sugden place the ridge beam over the plates and align the holes. "Place stinks like a thousand outhouses. Are we supposed to sleep in this crap? And I do mean crap."

A loud rumble had us all on our knees until we realized it was only one of the deuce-and-a-halfs starting up.

"Aw, for Pete's sake," Halloran muttered as we got to our feet, newly sticky from the shins down and looking sheepish.

"Wonder where they're going?" I said as we watched Lieutenant Duncan roll off with a handful of troops in the back of the truck.

We shrugged and fell quiet as Driscoll, who'd been assembling the mast poles, sunk one of them at the far end.

The rest of us grabbed a handful of canvas and pulled as he worked the pole into place at the other end. He quickly tied the beam to the plate with some rope so it wouldn't separate if a wind lifted the canvas after the tent was up. We each grabbed some poles and started placing them around the perimeter of the tent.

Ioli broke our silence. "Hey, Jon. Where would you rather be?"

"Saginaw, back home with the missus," Sugden said, placing a pole. "Lounging in the recliner, watching the Pistons whup the Knicks."

Ioli laughed and laid down another pole. "You wish!"

Driscoll picked up some stakes and the mallet. "I wish I was drag racing in the cornfields, me in my Mustang, tearing it up."

I thought of my car back home, Dad's old Pontiac I'd customized myself three years ago, just after I'd gotten my driver's license. Mary had promised to take good care of it while I was gone.

Halloran was cutting off lengths of rope for the stakes. "Dean," he piped up, "I bet you wish you were up on a stage somewhere, a-rockin' and a-rollin'."

"You know it," I said. *On tour with the Satellites.* My feet sank a little deeper. I took some rope from him and started looping it around the stakes Driscoll was driving into the mud. "I'd even take Captain's farewell gig."

Everybody broke out laughing.

What a joke that had been. The night before we shipped out from Fort Bragg, North Carolina, where they'd sent us after Fort Gordon, Leadbetter had thrown us a going-away party at the local enlisted club. Loaded us all onto trucks and shuttled us over. Right off the bat, I noticed a couple of amplifiers, guitars, and drums set up onstage. I thought we were going to have some music, so I was jazzed. We were all eating our farewell chow, laughing too loud, trying to hide how freaked out we were to be heading to Nam the next morning.

Then Leadbetter called me and Ioli and Voina over to his table. "Head for the stage," he commanded. "You guys are the show. Get up there and entertain."

We looked at him, at one another, our faces one big question mark. It was definitely an order. So we climbed onstage. Ioli's dad was a drummer once, he said, so he took the drums. Voina played a little guitar; he'd let me borrow his Stratocaster a few times back at Fort Gordon. He grabbed one of the guitars, I took the other. I wasn't sure how we were going to pull this off.

I knew Voina liked the old rock and roll, the simple stuff, like Elvis and Jerry Lee Lewis and Little Richard. "Okay, let's do every three-chord-run song we can think of," I told Voina, "just follow me." I called out a bunch of songs, chords, keys. "Johnny B. Goode." "Long Tall Sally." "Whole Lotta Shakin' Goin' On." "Great Balls of Fire." "Good Golly, Miss Molly." And our show closer, the one the guys liked best, "Wine, Wine, Wine."

Don't ask me how, but it worked. By party's end, we had the whole company—Captain too—in a frenzy, rocking and rolling on the tabletops. For the few guys old enough to drink, maybe the beers helped too. But when we were done, Leadbetter jumped up onstage and slapped us all on the back. "You guys were great!" he shouted over the whoops, hollers, and applause. "When we get to Vietnam, we're gonna do this some more! We're gonna put something together!"

Right.

"Man, y'all rocked," Halloran said, tying some rope from a stake to a tent pole.

"Thanks," I said, wondering when I'd ever touch a guitar again. "It sure beat another round of physical training." I squatted in front of a pole, preparing to lift.

"Yeah, running laps is for the birds," Ioli huffed as he fought for traction in front of a pole—and lost. He danced a little midair jig, then dropped in the glop—again.

By the time the company had all fifteen tents up, Duncan had returned, the truck piled high with wooden shipping pallets. We all gathered around.

"Pull 'em off and lay 'em down," Captain ordered. "Inside the tents, they'll get you up off the mud. Outside the tents, sidewalks, Nam style. All the comforts of home."

There were approving shouts and a ripple of applause.

I had to hand it to the captain. Rock concerts on the fly, floors in the middle of nowhere. He knew how to get things done. And he knew how to keep us busy, so we didn't think about where we were and why we were here. At least for the moment.

"We're losing the light!" Captain hollered as the last of the pallets went down. "Let's get on those sandbags!"

A groan went up as we grabbed shovels and empty burlap sacks from one of the trucks.

"More like mudbags," Sugden said as he and I worked together, filling and tying off sacks, then stacking them around the bottoms of the tents like the others. The bags were supposed to deflect enemy fire, but they were so wet and runny, I wasn't sure they could stop a bullet.

Great.

In minutes, the whole camp echoed with the rhythmic scrape of shovels, the squelching suck of the mud, and the *thuck* of one mud-filled bag after another being tossed onto the pile.

Anywhere else, I would've tried to set a tune to the beat. Here, it just didn't make any sense.

"You can be proud of yourselves, men."

We sat shoulder to shoulder on the pallet sidewalk that ran the length of our tent row. If Charlie was watching, he was probably laughing his butt off; we were a filthy, stinking, mud-encrusted bunch chowing on cold C-rations—

15

packaged nourishment that vaguely resembled food—in the darkening mist, empty weapons at our sides. And at that point, I couldn't have cared less. I was so tired, my bones ached. I was too bushed to be scared. Looking around, I guessed the others were feeling about the same way.

Except Captain, pacing among us as we ate. I wondered if he ever shut off.

"Tents are up and fortified, the perimeter secure. You followed orders and did what was asked of you. In a single afternoon, you built a camp from nothing, from no-man's-land, from a bulldozed sugarcane field. As you know, the 127th is a brand-new military police company, created for this very situation. You're pioneers, men. Mavericks. You are a credit to the army and your country. And in your honor I hereby christen this camp Dodge City."

I sure didn't feel like a cowboy.

The First Night

Captain was pacing again. Mud-streaked and puffing on his pipe as the light faded behind him, he looked like an old man. Of course, compared to our company, anybody would look old. Most of us hadn't even hit twenty-one yet. I'd turn twenty on January 25, just eighteen days away. Not that I was counting. Okay . . . I was. Twenty-eight down, three hundred thirty-seven to go. Uncle Sam started the meter the day we set foot on the ship.

"I need thirteen bodies on the perimeter. Nine on the inside. Two on the front gate. Two out front on the sandbag bunker."

Our first night of guard duty in Vietnam. Suddenly everyone was invisible, ducking heads, slouching low, looking at the ground. Man, those cots in the tent sounded good.

Leadbetter called out names anyway, and Lieutenant

Duncan marked them off on a clipboard. "McClory, Whitney, Lupica, Yoakum . . ." Guys grimaced, grabbed their flak jackets, steel pots (our metal helmets), and rifles, and set off for their posts.

"And out on the sandbags"—the rest of us winced— "let's see . . . Sherman. And Kohler."

Ham and lima beans flip-flopped in my gut.

"Sergeant Stallings will issue your ammo. Turn it back in to him at first light. Keep your eyes open out there, troops," Leadbetter said, and headed for his tent.

I didn't know Sherman all that well. I knew he was from Chicago, that he wasn't a whiner, and that he was pretty handy with the M79 grenade launcher at MP school. Stallings gave each of us two twenty-round magazines and a small metal box full of M14 rounds. I wondered if we'd need them as we snapped the first magazine into our rifles and shoved the other into our ammo pockets.

"Ready?" I asked, slinging my weapon over my shoulder and grabbing the ammo box.

"As I'll ever be." Sherman nodded and we trudged out.

By the time we got to our position—twenty yards beyond the front gate—the clouds were beginning to clear and the moon was up. Everything was quiet. Damp. Really hot. We'd been in Vietnam now for a whopping seven hours. We clutched our rifles behind the sandbags, every muscle tense, not knowing what to expect.

Waited.

Watched.

Listened.

Nothing. Just the drone of mosquitoes four times the size of the ones back home. Sounded like gunships coming in for a landing on your neck. We swatted them away and rubbed on more bug juice, but they kept coming. Now we knew why the army had us on malaria pills.

We waited and watched some more, straining to hear any sound, squinting into the dark.

Still nothing. It was eerily quiet, the air damp and heavy. The mud's stench filled my nostrils; I tried not to gag. Sweat poured into my eyes.

"I can't see a thing," Sherman whispered. He pulled off his pot and ran a palm over his face.

"Me neither," I whispered back. I took off my pot and wiped my eyes on my damp sleeve.

Still nothing.

We hadn't seen any of the enemy all day. Maybe there was no enemy out there. Our mission here in Qui Nhon was town patrol, law-and-order stuff. It wasn't like we were infantry, out crawling through the jungle looking for trouble.

Still, we were in a war zone. As if I could forget.

I swallowed hard and kept my eyes moving.

Sherman sat back on his pot.

"Hey, Dean," he whispered after a while, "you ever think you'd be doing this? Fighting in a war, I mean?"

Not in a million years.

Dad—retired navy officer, World War II vet, all sorts of medals and ribbons, survived the Battle of Coral Sea after his ship was sunk, treaded water with sharks for hours until he was rescued—*he* fought in a war.

Me, I tried to get out of it. Kind of. Didn't do what some wusses did, cop the daddy deferment, get hitched right out of high school and get the girl pregnant. Not worth screwing up Judy's life and an innocent kid's just to save my butt. Not worth running to Canada, either. I'm no coward.

But I did try the college deferment angle. Okay, so technically I wasn't in college, but I was registered for the coming semester at the local business school. My parents had already paid for it. So when the draft notice came—"Greetings from the president of the United States of America," like I'd won the sweepstakes or something—I drove straight down to the local draft board office and told them all about my big academic ambitions. Wasted breath.

I scanned the silvery blackness. "Nah, man. Never thought I'd be in a war."

Sherman was quiet. A gang of mosquitoes hovered near my cheek. I brushed them away.

"You got a girl back home?" Sherman whispered after a couple of minutes.

"Yeah," I said, not taking my eyes off the dark. "You?"

"Yeah," he said. "What's her name?"

20

"Judy." Her picture was at the bottom of my duffel. "Yours?"

"Sue Ann."

Sherman was silent a minute. "You love her?"

Good question. There was a time when I thought I did. Maybe not get-married-happily-ever-after love. But, yeah, Judy was cool, had a great body, we had fun together.

I thought of our many midnight telephone conversations. She'd wait until her mom was asleep, then close her bedroom door and call me. About a week after our first date, while we were talking, my parents came home from some big banquet at their Masonic lodge.

"We brought you some leftover donuts," Mom said as she gave me a kiss good night.

Judy had overheard her. "Bring me one," she purred into the phone.

"What?"

"Bring me a donut."

I laughed. "Are you crazy? It's almost one A.M. What if your mom wakes up?"

"Come on," she said. "Bring it to my bedroom window."

So I waited until my folks were asleep. I snuck out the back door and ran the three blocks to her house.

She was waiting in the window. I handed her the donut.

She took a bite and said, "Kiss me." Her lips were soft, sweet. We were a couple after that.

Then the draft notice came and changed everything.

"We left it pretty open-ended," I whispered. "A lot can happen in a year." Like your girl maybe finding somebody new. Like losing a record deal. Like getting your ass shot at.

Sherman nodded and pulled out a cigarette.

The instant he lit up, a gunshot whizzed between us.

We saw it before we heard it—a tall plume of dirt erupting from the embankment behind us, then the *z-z-zoosh* right between us. Sherman's eyes got so wide the whites glowed.

"Did somebody just . . . shoot at us?" The cigarette fluttered in Sherman's hand. He threw it down as if it had bitten him.

My brain went blank. But only for an instant.

We dropped to our bellies, rifles raised, frantically searching the dark. We knew not to shoot. Our muzzle blasts would only make us an easier target.

"You all right?" I hissed, tugging my helmet back on. Our first sniper fire. My stomach pinwheeled.

"I-I think so," Sherman panted. "Nothing hurts."

We heard a voice from our rear and swung our rifles around.

"Don't shoot! It's Vedlitz! Don't shoot!"

He'd seen us take the fire and was crawling through the mud to reach us. I thought of night-infiltration training back at basic, the full-speed body crawl under barbed wire, stream of machine-gun fire overhead, no room to think, just "Move! Move! Move!" *God bless drill sergeants.*

Vedlitz was huffing and puffing when he reached us. "You guys all right?"

"Yeah, we're good," I told him. My voice sounded strange, tight and high. "You see where it came from?"

"Had to have been down there." He pointed straight out beyond the bunker at the paddy now glimmering in the misty moonlight.

The three of us knelt behind the bags and scanned the rice field over our rifles. Nothing.

After a few minutes Vedlitz said, "I'm going back. Whatever you do, don't fall asleep."

Roger that.

Together, Sherman and I watched the night. Our first Nam night. The two of us huddled in the mire behind the sandbags. We stared out into the dark, curled up around our rifles, stomachs taut, afraid to breathe.

At dawn, a figure crawled out of the rice paddy.

"Look!" I yelped to Sherman. "Think that's our shooter?"

We signaled to the guys at the front gate to cover us and ran in the mud, M14s drawn. He was a skinny old man. Tiny, silver hair gleaming, wearing what looked like black pajamas, he carried baskets of rice, yoke-style, on a pipe across his shoulders.

Sherman jammed his gun's muzzle into Grandpa's back.

"What are you doing out here?" I yelled at the guy. Sherman and I didn't speak any Vietnamese. None of the 127th did. "Why are you here?"

It was like talking to a hole. No words, no expression. Just flinty eyes, staring at us.

"What are you doing here?" I repeated, slower and louder.

He stared.

I shook my head, then eyed the pipe on the old man's shoulders.

"You thinking what I'm thinking?" Sherman asked.

"That pipe would make a nifty rice-paddy zip gun?"

"Bingo."

We couldn't prove anything, though. We hadn't seen him shoot.

After patting him down and confiscating his pipe, we let him walk away, dragging his rice baskets behind him.

Was he on our side? Was he the enemy?

Who the hell could tell?

RETURN FIRE

The sun was barely up and the heat already stifling when Sherman and I trudged back to camp and turned in our ammo.

Somebody wanted me dead.

Maybe it was an old rice farmer. Maybe it was somebody else we couldn't see. Somebody I didn't know, somebody I'd never met, somebody with no idea of who I was or what I was all about had tried to kill me.

I replayed the night over and over in my mind like a reel-to-reel stuck on rewind. We should've been more alert. We should've paid attention. We should've known there'd be someone in the paddy. We should've . . .

Should we have shot back? The incoming fire was a single round. A snipe, not an all-out ambush. Returning fire would only have pinpointed our position. And if there were more than one shooter out there, it probably would've provoked something way more serious. No. We definitely did the right thing.

But something else kept nagging at me, picking at the back of my brain. Not *should* we have shot back, but *could* I have shot back. Target practice and endless drills and mock warfare out on the training field—all that was one thing. I'd aced my marksmanship tests—my rifle skills were excellent—but firing at a living, breathing person? That was something totally different.

Was that old man our sniper? He probably had a wife, kids, and grandkids, maybe even great-grandkids. He'd probably worked that rice paddy all his life. Maybe this was the family's land, where the old man's ancestors had farmed for centuries, where they were laid to rest in the cemetery. The cemetery we'd probably defiled by setting up camp nearly on top of it.

Maybe he dug music, like I did. Maybe he played an instrument. Maybe he loved his country and passed his patriotism on to his children, teaching them about duty and honor, just like Dad had taught me. Maybe he was defending his land, his nation, from foreigners he thought didn't belong here.

Maybe he wanted me dead.

Could I have killed him? Did I want *him* dead?

"Heard you handled yourself real well out there." Sergeant Stallings interrupted my thoughts. I handed him my magazines. "You're all set, Kohler. Check in with your platoon sergeant this afternoon. Now go get some rest."

"Catch you later, man," I mumbled to Sherman and headed to Three Squad's tent. I was spent, so bone-tired it felt like I was walking through quicksand.

I pulled back the flap. Except for a few snores and restless movements, the tent was quiet. My body exhausted and my mind numb, I dropped my rifle and tugged off my boots.

I tumbled onto my cot and slipped into a deep, empty sleep.

It was late afternoon when I woke up. It took me a few seconds to remember where I was. I was drenched in sweat and so was the green government-issue sheet on my cot. Mosquitoes feasted on my hands and face. I slapped at them and reached under the cot for the bug juice tucked in my helmet.

The tent was empty, but I could hear activity outside. I peeled off my crusty fatigues, releasing a shower of dried red mud shards that fell to the floor and disappeared between the pallet slats. I needed a shower—badly. I pulled some clean fatigues, socks, and underwear from my duffel and got dressed.

Squinting as my eyes adjusted to the glare, I stepped out into the brilliant sunlight. The camp was bustling, soldiers busy as worker ants. Directly across from the tent row, guys were staking off a GP Large, others loading tables and chairs into it. Had to be our new mess tent. Another group of guys was scooping heavy mud into sandbags and stacking them around the bottom of the tent. I could hear them complaining. Before last night, I would've been griping too. Not now. I'd take all the fortification I could get.

"Ah, Sleeping Beauty awakes." Sugden. He had a shovel in his hand. His dark hair was matted with sweat, his soaked T-shirt clung to his body like forest green plastic. "Man, I heard about last night. Got pretty hairy, huh?"

The whole camp was probably talking about it, and all I wanted to do was just forget it.

I ran a hand over the back of my head and tried to sound cool. "Yeah. Got shot at." Bits of mud had dried in my regulation buzz cut. For a second, I thought of the shaggy, long hair I used to have, the hair I'd shake over my guitar that made the girls in the audience scream. Gone in three swipes of the clippers at boot camp.

Sugden raised his eyebrows over his glasses. "What happened?"

"Just a sniper," I said, rubbing mud crumbles from my scalp. The old man's silver hair flashed into my mind. Dad had always been after me to cut my hair. "Single round. Surprised the hell out of us."

Sugden let out a low whistle. He leaned on the shovel and studied me, like I was a puzzle he was trying to solve. "You okay?"

I didn't want to talk about it anymore. I didn't want to

think about it anymore.

"Yeah, I'm fine." I raked some dried mud off my head and tossed it at him. "Just need to switch shampoos."

Sugden took the hint. He flashed a quick grin, hoisted the shovel, and slung it over his shoulder like a hobo's stick. "Come on, man. You've got to check this out."

I followed him down the pallet sidewalk.

"Looks like I missed all the fun," I said, pointing to the mess tent.

"That's not all," Sugden said, stopping between two GP Mediums. He pointed at thirty military jeeps parked in the mud. "New motor pool. Town patrols start tomorrow. They're teaming us with the outgoing MPs."

Terrific. My first interaction with the locals hadn't gone so well. What would town patrol bring? "Can't wait," I muttered. My mouth felt dry.

"Yeah, me too," Sugden said. "Guess it beats filling sandbags, though." We started walking again.

Sugden pointed beyond the mess tent. "Look over there." I could see a pair of large metal shipping containers, the kind that fit onto the back of a semi truck. "Our new ammo and supply sheds."

Definitely a surprise. But a good one. Back at Gordon and Bragg, the simplest things—getting new uniforms, requisitioning equipment—took forever. "Already?" I said. "This an army camp?"

As we neared the end of the pallets, I could see a couple

of crude structures. To the left was a simple lean-to made of two-by-fours and a plastic tarp, with a plywood bench inside. Holes—butt-sized holes—were sawn into the plywood. Metal oil drums cut in half sat under the holes.

"I give you . . . the latrine," Sugden said, waving his hand with a mock flourish.

"Nice," I snickered. "Phew! Smells like it's been broken in already. Or is that the mud?"

Sugden fanned the air in front of his nose, made a face, and turned toward the other structure. Sheets of plywood were fastened together into a screen. Corrugated metal tubing hung over it. My eyes followed the tubing back about fifty yards to a hillside, where I could just make out what looked like a small stream.

"And, behold . . . the shower," Sugden said. He reached over and opened a valve in the tubing. Brownish water trickled from a handful of perforations in the tin.

I chuckled. Back at training, we'd spent days, even weeks, out in the field with only water from our canteens to wet our faces and rinse our mouths. Now we were stuck in a stinking mud flat in the middle of Southeast Asia, but we had a shower stall with running water—such as it was. Pretty darn hilarious. And ingenious.

It felt good to laugh.

"Who came up with this idea?" I asked.

"Captain."

I shook my head and grinned. "Should've known."

We heard bootsteps behind us.

"Privates First Class Kohler and Sugden! Hate to bust up the coffee klatch, ladies, but there's work to do." Sergeant Hall, our platoon leader and the company's top sergeant, dropped a stack of empty burlap sacks at my feet. "Get shoveling."

There weren't any pallets in the mess tent—the floor was still mud—but we didn't care. The chow was propane-stove hot and hadn't come from a C-rat can, and the rain, which had resumed just minutes earlier, was falling on the roof, not on our heads. Closest thing to heaven we'd experienced in two days.

Word had spread through the company about the sniper fire, and the guys were asking a lot of questions. I let Sherman do most of the talking.

After we'd eaten, Captain entered, strode to the front of the mess tent and told us the patrol schedule we'd be following. Three shifts: 0800 to 1600, 1600 to midnight, midnight to 0800. Before each patrol, we would muster for a weapons-and-uniform inspection. Guard duty at camp would follow the same shifts.

Sugden pulled front-gate guard duty, 1600 to midnight. He shrugged and let out a loud belch.

I'd be heading to downtown Qui Nhon for town patrol at 0800.

I reminded myself to breathe.

NIGHT OPS

It sounded like thunder, and it rattled me right out of my cot.

At first I thought I was dreaming.

Then Sergeant Elmgreen, our squad leader, raced through the tent with a flashlight, yelling, "We're being hit! Get out! Get the hell out of here!"

It was a mad scramble in the dark, all of us fumbling frantically for our pots and flak jackets, pulling on boots, grabbing rifles.

The heavy thud, the screaming whistle, and then the earth-shaking rumble. Mortar fire.

I dashed outside with the rest, rifle raised.

"What's happening?" somebody screamed in the dark.

"Take cover! Take cover!" Sergeant Elmgreen hollered as explosions boomed somewhere beyond our camp.

I dived behind the sandbags with the others and stared

up at the sky. It looked like the Fourth of July. Tracers whizzed across the blackness, brightly glowing balls that seemed to hypnotize. I heard the pops. Small-arms fire. More whistling, and the ground shook. "Oh, Mama!" I heard somebody whimper. My heart pounded in my ears.

"Keep low!" Elmgreen ordered in a hoarse whisper. "Stay down and keep quiet!"

I could sense bodies near me, pressed up into the sandbags, but it was too dark to tell who they were. I listened to the artillery, tried to focus on the sound. It was close, definitely close. But none of it seemed to be landing near us.

I inched up and peered over the sandbags, following the tracers as they whisked over our camp. Whoever was firing was either a lousy shot or was aiming somewhere else, somewhere beyond Dodge City. Were we next?

I could hear other squads taking cover. The ground shimmied under us with every blast, yet we didn't seem to be taking any fire. I couldn't hear any shells landing near us. I scrunched down low. There were answering mortars now. They weren't coming from our camp. What was happening?

Keep cool, Kohler. Keep cool. I tried to breathe.

The ground was shaking. I was shaking. And my finger was trembling on the M14's safety, ready to flip it in an instant. That's when I remembered—we had no ammunition. It was all locked up. Only the perimeter guards on night duty—what, thirteen of them?—were truly armed. What if the Congs snuck in right behind us, ready to slit

33

our throats as we sat there, totally defenseless? *What a stupid way to run a goddamn war.*

I felt fingers on my arm and nearly jumped out of my skin.

"Who is it?" I hissed, trying to follow noise discipline.

"Dean, that you?" a voice whispered back. Ioli. *Thank you, God.*

"Yeah, man." My heart was racing.

"What's happening?" His voice sounded thin and panicky.

"I don't know." I tried to sound calm. "We're not armed, man, you know that?"

"Yeah." He moved closer. "If Charlie's coming for us, what are we gonna do?"

We jerked in unison as a round tore through the sky, louder, closer than the rest, and exploded with an ear-splitting crack—where? Sounded like just outside our back gate. *Holy crap.*

"Man, that was close," Ioli croaked.

We sunk down even lower, clutching our rifles, making ourselves as small as possible. I could feel Ioli trembling. Just like me.

Then we heard gunships swooping in, their rotor blades chopping through the noise. They dropped flares, and the tangled hillsides beyond our rear gate lit up in plumes of red and silver.

Now I could see the rest of the squad. Everyone was

pressed low in the mud—some guys with mouths hanging open as they looked at the sky. Others had ducked their heads and screwed their eyes shut. Halloran held his rifle with his knees, his hands over his ears as the mortars rumbled.

The choppers tilted away, leaving us in the dark. The flares in the distance were tiny pink bursts at the far end of the mountain, the tracers arcing from the choppers to the ground in a graceful stream.

"They're strafing," Ioli whispered.

My mouth went dry.

We heard bootsteps on the pallets, running toward us.

"Elmgreen, keep your squad cool!" I recognized Lieutenant Duncan's voice. "It's the transportation unit down the road—they're taking fire and hitting back. Captain's got 'em on the radio."

So we weren't the only sorry souls out here in the mud? Looked like Charlie didn't want them—or us—in his backyard.

"Are we going in to assist, sir?" Sergeant Elmgreen asked.

Assist? Our whole squad held their breath.

"No, man. Choppers should be taking care of it. Captain wants your platoon's Two Squad and Four Squad on the fence the rest of the night, though, just in case. Everyone else can hit the racks."

I could almost hear the collective sigh of relief.

"You heard him," Elmgreen growled at us. "Everybody back in the tent."

I couldn't sleep the rest of the night. I don't think anybody did.

Listening to the fighting off in the distance, which came only sporadically now, I felt alone. Very alone. Even with eleven other guys shoehorned into a cramped tent, tossing in their cots just like me.

I turned over and lay still and flat. Stared up into the pitch black.

I thought about Mom, about how much I missed her. What would she say if she were here now?

Mom was always telling me I could do whatever I set my mind to. Even when I was little, all those years when Dad was out to sea most of the time and it was just me, Mary, and Mom. She was the one who had encouraged me when I started liking art, and I'd ended up winning awards all through school for my drawing and painting. I'd been the 127th's graphics guy since Sergeant White set me to work making all of his charts and diagrams back at Gordon. And the music—I was playing for cash within two years of begging Mom for guitar lessons at the Tony Saks Music Center.

Music was in my blood—because it was in Mom's blood. Grandma played harmonica, and Aunt Jean and all four of Mom's brothers played guitar and sang. Uncle Roy was so good that he and his band had their own TV variety show back home in Portsmouth—you could hear their music on the radio. And when Roy had come back from New York

City with the Satellites' record deal, Mom had been as thrilled as I was.

The record deal. I squeezed my eyes shut and shoved it out of my mind. My throat hurt.

Mosquitoes whirred next to my ear. I waved them away with an angry swipe.

I thought of Dad. About how he'd always been after me to lay off the rock and roll and get a real job. Which in Portsmouth meant one of two things after high school: joining the navy, or going to work at the shipyard.

As graduation got close, I'd tried to imagine myself in a hard hat shuffling through the shipyard gates every day to scrape rust, weld hulls, rivet boilerplates. For Dad's sake, I really tried. But I just couldn't do it.

Funny. Now I could get shot at or blown up at any moment. *So this is a real job, right, Dad?*

Dad had been pleased to see me go. He wasn't much of a talker. I saw it in his eyes when he looked at me in my freshly creased dress uniform the day I shipped out, the way he embraced me—not like a kid but like a man. "Write as often as you can," was all he told me. He thought the army—going to war—would be good for me.

And in a way, I was happy to go too. Dad had done what his country had asked of him. It was what a man—a real man—did.

And now it was my turn.

THE PX

Morning dawned hot and bright. And hot.

I grabbed some chow—reconstituted eggs and sausage patties—then stopped by the shipping-container-turned-ammo-depot to get issued a .45 pistol and ammo and headed for formation at 0800. The jumble of voices fell away as Sergeant Hall called us to attention and read names from his roster. Then he conducted the inspection, walking up and down the ranks, checking our weapons and uniforms.

"Kohler, you and McClory are partners today," he said, eyeballing the sleeves of my green utility shirt for evenness and checking that my hair wasn't touching my ears. He scrutinized my web belt, looking for ammo, handcuffs, nightstick, and holster, and checked that I was wearing the dark blue MP helmet and not my green steel pot. He snatched my rifle from my hands and looked it over, making sure it was cleaned and oiled. "You'll be riding with

Specialist Washington of the 177th MP Company today," he said as he tossed me the rifle and examined my pistol. "He's waiting for you guys out at the motor pool."

Hall dismissed us, and McClory—a stocky Louisianan who only seemed to speak when necessary—gave me a nod as we walked out to the jeeps.

Washington was a wiry black guy with a friendly handshake. "You even old enough to be in a war?" he asked me, grinning and pumping my hand. "Looks like you's all of fifteen years old."

I heard it all the time.

"Baby Face," McClory said. "That's what we called him back at training."

I rolled my eyes. "And we call McClory here the Clam. He doesn't talk much—usually."

The specialist chuckled. "Well, you can call me Wash," he said as we climbed into his jeep, McClory in back, me riding shotgun. "Leave it to ol' Wash to show you new guys the lay of the land."

We pulled out of the red mud at Dodge City and Wash swung the jeep onto a thin strip of road. It surprised me that, out here in the middle of nowhere, the road was paved.

I mentioned it to Wash. "Yeah," he said, "Army Corps of Engineers did their number on Qui Nhon last year, back when they decided it was gonna be a deep-draft port to offload supplies. Used to be a fishing village. Now it's like the Newark of Nam, you know? Everything comes into Qui

Nhon. Napalm, Pepsi-Cola, RCA TV sets. They get dropped on the docks and sent out to all the military in-country."

The land around us was flat and open. Behind it, humble hills bowed to craggy mountains looming in the distance. Paddies whizzed by on one side of the road, neat squares marked by low stone dikes. I pointed to the rows and rows of gleaming green stalks on the other side. "What's that? The tall stuff?"

"Sugarcane," Wash said, smacking his lips and drumming his fingers on the steering wheel. "Nature's lollipop, man. Peel back the outside, suck on the middle. Mmm-mmm. That's the good stuff."

We passed by some locals, the first Vietnamese I'd seen other than the old man. Looked like a family, an old woman all stooped over; a younger woman, black hair down her back; two kids. All of them tiny, everybody wearing those pajamas. And straw hats. Cone-shaped, like a lamp shade or something. They were walking barefoot in a paddy, driving a water buffalo with a long stick.

As we flew by, they looked up for a moment and the children waved. Without thinking, I waved back.

It all seemed so tranquil, so harmless, like a picture out of a social-studies textbook. Where was the war?

"You guys get much contact?" I asked. "See any Viet Cong?"

Wash shook his head. "Naw, it ain't like the grunts up north or inland, they got it bad. See, we're wall-to-wall military. Army, navy, air force—they all got real estate here in Qui Nhon. So we're pretty well-defended." He pointed to the jagged horizon. "You got your Korean Tiger Division in tanks just over the mountains there. Infantry farther out on jungle duty." Then he jerked a thumb in the opposite direction. "Navy jets on carriers on the water ready to drop bombs. They all makin' sure no VC get into the city."

I liked the sound of that.

"Kohler took some fire the other night," McClory piped up from the backseat.

Wash glanced over at me. "That right?"

I glared at McClory, then softened. Maybe it had spooked him too. "Just a snipe." I tried to sound casual. "Guard duty. Might've been this old guy in a paddy. Hard to tell."

Wash turned off the main drag onto a smaller road. I could see a low-slung building not too far in front of us. "Ol' Charles, he sneaky," Wash said. "Gets to the townsfolk when you ain't watchin' and turns 'em. And everybody's all lookin' the same, so you can't never tell who's who. Trust no one, that's what the army tells us. We heard Qui Nhon was crawlin' with Congs when the army first got here. That mountain behind your camp? Blasted with Agent Orange a couple years back—or so's they say."

"No way," I said. McClory's eyes got big.

"Yessirree," Wash said. He tapped out another rhythm on the steering wheel. "We get a sniper here and there, we surely do. But things is really heating up about a hundred miles from here, up toward An Khe and Pleiku, the highlands, the front lines. Congs is blowing up the bridges, man, big-time, just as fast as the Corps is rebuilding 'em. That's where they sendin' us next week, the whole company. So you guys is takin' our place." Wash shook his head. "Can't say I'm looking forward to it, being halfway through my time already."

"Tough break, man," I said. So maybe Dodge City wasn't all bad. Sure sounded better than stuff blowing up.

Wash shook his head again and clicked his tongue. "You ask me, I say this here's the safest place in the whole damn war. The Congs ain't gonna blow up Qui Nhon, 'cause they want to steal all our goodies, all the food and ammo and Pepsis. No Qui Nhon, no stuff to steal. Plus, they more interested in a place like Saigon. You gonna blow something up, you do it there, with all the news cameras. Get some real publicity for your bombing buck, know what I mean?"

Wash pulled up in front of the building. A small fleet of military jeeps and trucks was parked out front.

"This here's your PX," he said, shutting off the engine and hopping out. "Come on, I need a case of Pepsis."

We followed him in. Now this was more like it. Aisles and aisles of anything a civilized soldier could need. Toiletries, candy, canned food items. Books and magazines. Cameras, radios. The smell of french fries and cheeseburgers wafted from a large snack bar in the back.

We split up and wandered the aisles. Just seeing the

familiar packages put me in a good mood. Hershey's bars in the dark brown wrapper. A rainbow of Kool-Aid packets, every flavor under the sun. Bars of Ivory soap in crisp waxed wrappers. It was the closest thing to home I'd seen in over a month.

I grabbed two cans of chocolate macaroons, my favorite, from the food aisle. Wash hoisted a case of Pepsi-Cola onto his shoulder. McClory, fingering a six-pack of Juicy Fruit, and I followed Wash to the cashier.

Along with his MPCs—the military "Monopoly money" we'd been told to use here—Wash pulled a small card out of his wallet. "See this? This is your ration card. You'll be getting one yourselves. You got all these little squares on it, see? And when you buy a rationed item, they punch out a square."

"Rationed items?" I asked. "Like what—food? Metal?"

"More like stuff that guys can buy here and resell downtown on the black market. Take this case of Pepsi. Two-forty here at the PX, right? Well, it's worth fifteen, maybe even twenty bucks downtown."

"No kidding?" I said.

"All true," Wash said, handing his card to the clerk.

McClory looked puzzled but didn't say anything as he paid for his gum.

"So what else is rationed?" I asked, handing the cashier some MPCs for my cookies.

"Either of you smoke?" Wash said.

We shook our heads.

"Well, if you did, you're allowed four cartons of cigarettes a month." Wash grabbed his case of sodas and we headed out the door. "Everybody's allowed one camera per tour. And everybody's allowed one stereo."

A stereo? In a war? Man, what wouldn't I give for a little music.

We hopped back in the jeep. Wash started it up and threw it in reverse.

"Next stop, downtown Qui Nhon," he said.

QUI NHON

It looked like Academy Park, back home in Portsmouth, the neighborhood Mom called "the wrong side of the tracks." Only twenty times worse.

Mounds of dilapidated tires. Heaps of trash. Bits of scavenged plywood and cardboard and Coca-Cola tin-can scraps held together with chicken wire. And people were living inside the rickety garbage piles, barefoot kids playing outside in the mud. The locals looked up, empty-eyed, as we passed by.

"Man, that's rough," I said. McClory sat silent and blinking in the backseat.

"Things ain't so easy for the locals these days," Wash said. "Especially the little ones, the babysans. Papasan off fighting with the ARVN, Army of the Republic of Vietnam—they's the ones with us—if he ain't a Cong. Mamasan and the grandparents tryin' to hold things together best they can. Not that things was ever easy in this place. These just the outskirts of town. Folks is pretty poor around here."

I could tell we were getting closer to the city itself when traffic picked up, a lot of American military jeeps and trucks. But mostly Vietnamese—on bikes, on tricycle rickshaws, on motor scooters. Some were piled on three and four people at a time.

"This here's Vo Tanh Street, the main drag," Wash said as he turned onto a busy avenue and wove his way through the rickshaws. Tiny, open-front stores were lined up on each side of the street like a hundred books on a shelf. All sorts of people milled around. Vietnamese in their cone hats, others in ARVN uniforms holding rifles. School-age children, some even younger, running alongside the military vehicles, waving postcards, trinkets, and cigarettes, and chirping, "You buy, GI!" Americans in uniform. Westerners in civilian clothes.

"Busy place," I said. I guessed kids didn't go to school here or play much tag or hide-and-seek.

"Yep, this is it," Wash said. "You got the locals, you got the GIs, you got all the contractors and longshoremen. And we MPs get to keep 'em all in line."

Great.

Wash kept moving, laying on the horn and shouting, *"Di-di!"* and, *"Di-di mau!"* at the traffic.

"What does that mean?" I asked. I leaned forward in my seat, craning my neck to take it all in.

46

Wash laughed. "They didn't teach you? *Di-di*—that's Vietnamese for 'go away.' *Di-di mau*—that's 'go away quickly.' You guys gonna need to know those. Here's some more. *Dung lai*—that means 'stop.' You gonna be using that one a lot. *Chop-chop*—that's 'eat.' Number one, that means 'the best,' and number ten, that means 'the worst.' And then there's *boom-boom*." Wash grinned. "You can probably figure that one out yourself."

I looked back at McClory. "You got all that?" He smiled and nodded.

Downtown was a multicolored mishmash of signs, cheesy store facades, and merchandise. As the jeep crawled through the congestion, we could see all sorts of vendors out on the sidewalks selling anything you could think of—clothing, produce and fish, live ducks and chickens, jewelry, transistor radios, smoking supplies, used tires, even monkeys.

"Looks like a flea market after a few pots of coffee," I joked.

"You know it," Wash said, swerving to avoid a flock of chickens in the street.

And it stank. What was it about Vietnam—everything stank? Downtown smelled like, well, crap. I figured it came from the chickens—and the dogs and the pigs—running loose everywhere. Then I saw it and couldn't believe my eyes. The locals were stopping and—squatting—right there on the sidewalk, in the open, in front of everybody.

"Tell me they're not doing what I think they're doing," I said to Wash.

"'Fraid so. You definitely gotta watch your step around here."

"Terrific," I muttered.

Wash pulled up in front of a large white building with an orange tile roof, like what you'd see in Mexico. Chain-link and razor wire surrounded the building and a sign over the front gate read MILITARY POLICE STATION—OFFICE OF THE PROVOST MARSHALL.

"This here's the downtown station," Wash said as an MP waved him through the gate. "This is where you'll report for a briefing at the start of every town-patrol shift. At the end of every shift, you come back here, turn in your traffic tickets, fill out your incident reports."

Wash parked the jeep and showed McClory and me around, then introduced us to some of the guys at the station. After the briefing, we hit the road again, Wash giving us his crash course in town patrolling. He took us over to the airbase, where massive C-130s lumbered down the runway to deliver supplies to the guys in the highlands, on the front lines. He showed us the intersections around the airbase where we'd be playing traffic cop, directing the melee of military vehicles, civilians on bikes and rickshaws, animals, and pedestrians. He showed us the key bridges the Corps had built all around the city, over paddies and streams. "Congs, they love the bridges," Wash told us. "Ain't never tried to blow up any in town—yet."

He took us down by the water, to the mile-and-a-half causeway and steel piers the Corps of Engineers had installed when it was decided Qui Nhon would be a logistical base. All sorts of vessels sat in the glittering blue bay—bobbing sampans, tankers offloading fuel, landing craft bringing equipment to shore.

Wash swung by the fuel depots, huge tanks filled with oil, then we headed downtown. He showed us which bars were off-limits to GIs, places where there'd been shootings or stabbings or where the army thought the owner was cozy with the Congs. Wash showed us how to check GIs for passes allowing them to be in town. It was my first time inside of a real bar; I wasn't old enough to drink back home.

Wash introduced us to the Rex, a dark, dirty little tavern that was a favorite with the Americans. He added, "Oh, one more thing about the bars: Some of them . . . well, guys don't go there just to get a drink from the waitress, if you know what I mean."

Oh. Okay. I got it. I smirked. "Boom-boom?"

Wash laughed. "You got it, Baby Face. Boom-boom. And I think I'll let you guys figure those bars out for yourselves. So, anybody up for a cheeseburger at the PX?"

We walked out of the PX with full stomachs and a second wind. The sun was high in the sky, and it felt about twenty degrees hotter than when we had gone inside.

And then we froze.

An army truck was idling in the parking lot. Other MPs were using it for cover, their guns drawn. A soldier in green fatigues was hanging out the passenger door, upside down, arms dangling on the pavement. The back of his head had been blown completely off. The truck's windshield was spattered with blobs of red gore. A chunk of something gray sat in a pool of blood on the dusty asphalt.

Oh, God, oh, God, oh, God.

My stomach lurched, and I tried not to throw up.

For a few moments, nobody moved. Then more MPs emerged from the bushes across the road, shaking their heads. They gave the all-clear, and an army ambulance pulled up. The medics unzipped a body bag.

Wash knew one of the MPs. "Towson, what happened?" I heard him ask.

"Sniper, man. Kid didn't even know what hit him."

The tent was quiet, everyone out on duty or patrol except for Driscoll, who was cleaning his weapon. He gave me a nod as I walked in.

"How was it?" he asked.

"Okay." I lay down on my cot.

"Town patrol?"

I put an arm up over my forehead. "Yeah." I wanted to talk to him. To someone. But I didn't know what to say. So I didn't say anything.

I guess he could tell I wasn't in the mood for company. He reassembled his rifle, put away the LSA—lubricant, small arms—and headed for the flap. Out of the corner of my eye I could see him pause for a moment. Then he shrugged.

"See you, man," he said.

"Yeah, see you."

Lying there in the green glow, I didn't know what to think or feel. It was only my third day in Vietnam.

I thought maybe I should write a letter home. Mom would be worried until she heard from me. Maybe it would make me feel better.

I reached under my cot and pulled a piece of blue USO stationery and a ballpoint pen from my pack.

Dear Mom and Dad, I began.

I couldn't think of what to write next. I tapped the pen slowly on my chin.

Wanted you to know that I'm okay.

Or maybe not.

Vietnam is—

Smelly. Hot. Disgusting. Scary. Deadly. Hot.

—different.

Yeah, where else can you get shot at, nearly ambushed, and see a kid with his brains blown out, all in three fun-filled days?

I lay back down. My stomach felt like it was on simmer.

Why am I so wigged out? I wondered. It wasn't the first time I'd seen a dead person up close. My great-grandmother died when I was eleven. My parents took me to her funeral. She'd been laid out in a satin-lined coffin in her Sunday best. Surrounded by all the flowers, she looked serene, like she was sleeping.

Today—that was close. Too goddamn close. Bloody. Messy. Ugly. That soldier with his brains baking on the sandy road, he was my age. Wearing the same uniform as me. Taken out while I sat stuffing my face right inside the PX. A few more seconds and that could just as easily have been me.

I tried to swallow.

Training doesn't prepare you for this.

HAPPY BIRTHDAY

The tent flap opened and one of the mess cooks walked in. He was carrying a cake, four layers, with white frosting and coconut on top.

"Happy birthday, man," he said, and handed me the cake. "Captain says enjoy your day off." He flashed me a peace sign and left.

My birthday. I'd forgotten all about it. The two and a half weeks since we'd arrived had flown by. In addition to our patrols and guard duty, Captain Leadbetter had us doing work details around the camp. It seemed like he was intent on turning Dodge City into our own little mountain-view resort.

First, there was electricity. One day a huge generator arrived on the back of a truck at the rear gate. Word was Captain had "appropriated" it somehow, since the army hadn't provided us one, and didn't intend to either. We unloaded the monster generator, set it up at the back of the camp, and, like magic, we had juice for the whole place. With a yank of a chain we had lights in the tents, and fans too.

Then there was the shower. Somehow, somewhere, Leadbetter'd requisitioned a pump, which he had us submerge in an old well we found on the company grounds. Soon we had clean, clear water running to a gravity-fed, sun-warmed holding unit above the shower stalls. Nice.

Within two weeks of our arrival, Captain had approved Vietnamese civilians working at Dodge City. House Mouses, we called them. Mamasans, none of them more than four and a half feet tall, who'd squat over buckets polishing our brass. They'd lug our laundry to the stream and scrub out our uniforms, even our olive-drab GI underwear. Their children, round-faced, smiling, begging for *chop-chop*, would shine our boots. Each soldier paid them five bucks a month. At first I was uneasy about bringing Vietnamese into the camp, but I figured Captain knew what he was doing. "Trust no one" was the rule—except if they were willing to do your grunt work.

Leadbetter had us replacing all the tents in the compound with wooden structures we built ourselves. These weren't any bogus, half-baked hooches, either. These were the real deal, with cement footings and everything. It definitely wasn't what the army had in mind for us; it was all Leadbetter's idea. And, man, we loved him for it. We couldn't wait to get out of our dripping-wet tents, guys on top of one another in the mud, the clammy uniforms, the soggy sheets.

Mess hall was the first building up, then the orderly room, the camp's "office" where the first sergeant took care of paperwork for things like payroll and passes and requisitions and inspections. The bar was the third building up. We were just getting started on the first of the barracks. Captain planned a long row of them, two stories. They were going to be simple frame structures, a tin roof on top, screening for the walls to keep the bugs out, and wooden jalousie louvers along the lower half for a little privacy. Sandbags, of course, around the bottom to deflect enemy fire. Since I was the art guy in the company, Leadbetter had me painting the signs for every one of the new buildings. He named the bar the Longbranch Saloon and had me do up the inside with pictures of surfers and cartoon characters.

I didn't mind all the work. I liked keeping busy. It kept my mind off other stuff. Like what I was missing back in "the world." Like what was going on here.

"You gonna eat that?" Ioli asked. "Oh, and happy birthday, dude, I mean that."

I could practically see his mouth watering.

Sugden thumped me on the back. "Yeah, happy birthday, man. You deserve a day off. So"—he smacked his lips—"you're going to eat that all by yourself?"

I ran a finger through the frosting and stuck it in my mouth.

Ioli and Sugden stood transfixed, like puppies begging for a treat.

I pointed at Ioli's face. "Mike, man, you've got a little drool on your chin," I teased.

They clobbered me, slapping at my head and arms. "All right, all right!" I laughed, nearly dropping the cake. "Geez, let's go to the mess hall and knock this thing out."

A day off. I hardly knew what to do with myself.

I wandered around the camp a bit, watching Sergeant Hall supervise a handful of old Vietnamese men and women as they dug holes that would be footings for the new barracks. They jabbered away in their high, shrill voices, Sergeant Hall trying to show them what he wanted with exasperated "number tens" and "number ones." At first, I'd felt kind of sorry for the Vietnamese doing all of our chores for us. But every morning they lined up at the front gate, looking for work. Our five bucks a month was probably more than they made all year.

Someone was sitting on the pallet sidewalk outside of Two Squad's tent. I walked over. McConnell. He had an enormous grasshopper, at least six inches long and fluorescent green, pinned down in front of him with one hand. With the other, he was trying to tie a piece of string around the grasshopper's body. An empty gallon-sized mayo jar from the mess hall sat on the sidewalk next to him, a handful of holes punched through its lid.

"What the hell are you doing?" I asked him.

"Keepin' it for a pet. Gimme a hand, would you? His leash ain't goin' on too well."

"That's crazy," I said, but I knelt down and held the giant insect for him.

"Hey, Kohler!"

Dersheimer stuck his head out of Four Squad's tent. "Come here a second."

Dersheimer was from Florida, a pro water-skier at Cypress Gardens before he got drafted. He was sitting on his cot, flipping a big, red, fiberglass-coated circle in his hand.

"What's that thing?" I asked.

"A ski disc," he said proudly. "You water-ski on it."

"Where'd you get it?"

"I met some navy guys out on patrol the other day," he said. "We started talking about skiing, they had some marine plywood in the shop, and they made it for me."

He sounded so matter-of-fact. It was funny how we MPs were learning how to get things done. Leadbetter must've been rubbing off on us.

Dersheimer flipped the disc over to me like a Frisbee.

I caught it and gave it a whirl on my fingertips. "What do you want me to do with it?"

He grinned. "Paint a Snoopy on water skis on it."

I thought about it for a second, then shrugged. I had nothing better to do.

We headed over to the shipping container that now served as our supply depot, and I pulled out an assortment of paints. I sketched Snoopy hopping a speedboat's wake, skis on his feet, one arm raised in a wave. Then I painted it in. Dersheimer loved it.

We took it outside to dry in the sun. Pelton, the mail clerk, called us over to the shipping container he'd turned into the mail room.

"Got a package for you, Kohler," he said. He handed over a large box wrapped in brown paper. It was from Mom.

I opened it up right there. It was loaded with all sorts of goodies. A couple of jars of Tang; small boxes of Rice Krispies and Frosted Flakes, the single-serve kind; cans of my favorite mac and cheese and beef stew; a tin of home-made chocolate-chip cookies; a big jar of Ovaltine. At the bottom was a stack of music magazines, *Hit Parader*, *Tiger Beat*, *Song Hits*.

There was a card. I took my time opening it. Mail had been slow getting here; I'd only gotten two other letters—one from Mom and one from my cousin Cecil—and we'd been here almost a month. I wanted to savor it.

> *Dear Dean,*
>
> *I hope this makes it to you in time for your birthday. We watch the TV news every night, hoping that you are safe.*
>
> *The magazines are from Mary. She says to tell*

you that your car is fine.

I ran into Judy at the drugstore the other day. I gave her your address so she could write you. I hope that was the right thing to do.

We miss you terribly and can't wait until you come home so we can all celebrate your 21st birthday together.

Love, Mom

I reread the card a few more times, then carefully put it back in the box and carried the whole thing to Three Squad's tent. I slid the box under my cot, behind my duffel. For a second I thought I was going to cry.

"Hey, Kohler!" Dersheimer poked his head into the tent. He had the ski disc in his hand. "It's dry and I don't have patrol till tonight. Come on, man, let's take it to the beach. I gotta try this thing out."

I had the whole day off. Why not? Sure beat sitting around Dodge City feeling sorry for myself.

We grabbed some passes from Sergeant Hall and got a lift from one of the guys working motor pool.

The beach. Vietnam's best-kept secret. For the most part, wish-you-were-here strands of golden sand and shimmering blue water, fishermen's sampans nodding and dipping in the distance. For the other part, glad-you're-not stretches of dead fish and garbage. We steered clear of "Shit Beach" and got dropped off at the harbor.

I hung around on the pier, and damned if the navy guys didn't pull Dersheimer around on that thing with one of their swift boats. I wouldn't have believed it if I hadn't seen it.

Then they went "grenade fishing." Toss a concussion grenade in the water and the fish come right up to the top.

A brutal sport for a brutal place.

"Bridge Nine's hit! Grab your gear! Move! Move! Move!"

I jumped from my cot, rubbing my eyes. The lights were on and Elmgreen was screaming through the tent.

I yanked on clammy fatigues and boots. Grabbed my helmet, rifle, and flak jacket and hurried into the drizzle with the rest. Three Squad piled into a three-quarter-ton truck and hurtled through the misty blackness to what was left of the bridge.

We were learning that the nights belonged to the Cong.

The rubble smoldered, orange in the wet. Smoke stung my eyes and burned my nose. I thought of Wash. He'd told us Charlie loved the bridges.

"Move out and drop!" Elmgreen yelled. "Go! Go! Go!"

We crouched in the paddies, sunk to our waists in the stinking mud, guns out of the water. Everything was wet, everything was black. Suddenly we heard popping noises. I could see muzzle flashes in the dark, on the far side of where the bridge used to be. We all dove into the slime and my heart felt like it was thumping all over my chest.

"Open fire! Open goddamn fire!" Elmgreen screamed.

M14s erupted around me, their deafening chatter rattling my skull. And suddenly I was angry. Angry at this place, the smell, the heat, mosquitoes, and flies. And mud and more mud.

Angry at being scared.

I'd already squeezed off rounds before my brain told me to do it. The enemy fired back at us, ammo whizzing and glowing above us like fireflies. Across the burned-out bridge, the flashes moved, the enemy changing position as we returned fire.

A round whined past my ear so close I could smell the powder, the rotten-egg blaze. Another round hit close by, sending a spray of swampy water down my neck. Then another. And another. Bursts of gunfire volleyed over the paddy, echoing in my ears.

And I was still alive.

It was strange. Exciting. I'd never felt anything like it. I was too strong. Too well-trained. Too damn *American* to be done in by a bunch of pajama-wearing rice farmers with machine guns. I was bulletproof. Superman.

Somebody was screaming. A ragged, gargling sound, loud at first and then it faded away under the noise. One of us? One of them?

The gunfire kept coming. We kept shooting.

We shot into the night.

The night shot back.

With the first sunlight, the shots slowed down. And then stopped. And then they were gone.

Two of the bridge guards we'd come to help were wounded. One had taken a round in the shoulder, the other a hit that had shattered his knee. I didn't know the guys; they were from a different company. But I felt bad for them. And I felt bad that a part of me was glad that it hadn't been me. Their buddies carried them to our truck and loaded them onto the back.

Elmgreen had us walk the paddy, looking for kills. There were blood-streaked tracks in the mud—where the enemy had dragged away their injured, we figured. And then we saw them, the men intent on killing us. Except they were dead. Five of them. Facedown in the mud, bodies bent. One had his arm outstretched—behind him, fingers to the sky— as if he wanted to ask a question.

Some of the guys gave cheers. Others were quiet.

I was just following orders.

I was twenty years old. Happy birthday to me.

Prisoner Patrol

"I'm telling you, man, it ain't pretty," Driscoll said from behind the wheel as we headed to the 67th EVAC hospital next to a supply company out near the airport.

It was early February and I was on prisoner patrol. "What, the VC get brave or something? They try to pull stuff?" My hand went instinctively to my holster.

"No, man, they're all pretty messed up," Ioli said from the back of the jeep. "They ain't goin' nowhere. The ugly part's our guys. The grunts from the field, you know?"

"What about 'em?" I asked.

Driscoll shook his head. "Every day those medevac Hueys bring 'em in and drop 'em off and they're all tore up six ways to Sunday. You'll see."

I thought they were playing with me, trying to scare me or something. The three of us walked past rows and rows of low cement buildings. "The wards," Driscoll said. "That one there on the end, with all the barbed wire around it, that's where they keep the VC."

We checked in with the guys we were relieving and took our positions, Ioli at the prison ward's front gate, Driscoll in the back, me inside.

"It's pretty easy duty," Driscoll said before he left me. "The Congs just lie around with their arms blown off or something. They won't bother you."

And then it was just me and the enemy. I wandered the long rows of beds. The ward smelled of Lysol and fish. Driscoll was right—most of the prisoners were pretty helpless, unconscious or nearly out of it, missing limbs or with their heads wrapped up in bandages. Those who seemed alert stayed quiet, their dark eyes following me around the room. It gave me the creeps.

"Hey, MP," a hoarse voice called out from the back row of beds. I nearly jumped. The voice was American.

I paced the back row. Americans, in every bed. Skinny and haggard, some with arms and legs and feet missing, others with eyes patched over or faces that looked like they'd melted away. Some looked older, in their midtwenties, but most of them seemed around my age, one or two maybe even younger. It was hard to tell with their eyes shut. Something squeezed tight around my heart.

Finally, I found him. He looked a little older than me, with light brown hair and tired blue eyes. His left hip was buried in a mound of gauze. He had a tube in his nose, and a hose ran from a bag hanging high on a hook into his arm.

"Talk to me," he said. "I don't like lying here with all these gooks."

I'd never liked that word for the Vietnamese. It sounded so . . .

He asked me my name.

"Kohler. Dean Kohler. What happened?" I asked, shaking his hand.

"Booby trap. Charlie got me but good." He closed his eyes and chuckled weakly. "Blew off half my ass."

I winced. "Why do they have you in here, then, with the enemy?"

"I don't know, Kohler. Guess they ran out of room in the ICU." His faded eyes narrowed. "Could be one of these sonofabitches planted the trap that got me."

I shook my head because I didn't know what to say.

"Crafty bastards," the guy went on, obviously grateful for someone to listen to him. "It was a grenade, out in the boonies near Pleiku. Jungle land." Wasn't that where Wash said his company had been headed? "We were running ambushes up there, at night. I didn't see a goddamn thing. Pin was pulled. They rigged it with a trip wire and stuffed it into an old C-rat can. I was lucky, man, my pack took most of the blast. Shrapnel sure carved up my butt, though."

He seemed to want to talk about it, so I told him about the booby traps some of our guys had come across the other day out on patrol in the Valley, the low terrain just inland of Qui Nhon.

"Three or four pieces of steel rod with a barbed hook on each end," I described. "Looked like those twirly things in a kid's game of jacks, only twenty times the size. All scattered in the high grass."

The guy nodded. "Yeah, we saw those out in the boonies too. Congs toss 'em around. No matter where they land there's always a sharp point sticking straight up, waiting for some sorry soldier to come along and step on it. Rusty point busts right through the bottom of your boot, into your foot." He stopped to clear his throat. "Hey, can you hand me my water?"

I handed him a paper cup with a straw in it from his bedside table. He took a sip and went right on talking. "And with that damn hook, you can't pull the thing out. Either got to push it through the rest of the way, or cut a bigger goddamn hole in your foot to back it out. That's some nasty business, there." He paused for a moment, then lifted a finger and waved it around. "Yeah, these assholes got all of us doing the booby-trap shuffle, huh? We got 'em back good, though. Look at 'em now." He let out a wheezy sort of laugh. I found myself laughing too, and it surprised me.

A cute nurse, blond, nice figure, came in.

"You're not keeping Sergeant Joynes here from his rest now, are you, Private?" She opened up a brown bottle of peroxide and poured it out onto a large wad of cotton.

"No, ma'am," I said.

"Nurse Smart, my lovely ray of sunshine," Joynes said. "We were just comparing notes, the MP and I. Good to talk to somebody who speaks English, you know?"

The nurse lifted the mound of gauze and I could see a hole the size of a football in Joynes's hip. It looked like raw, red meat, crisscrossed with thick, black stitches. Yellow fluid oozed into the hole. I wondered what the wound would look like when it healed—if it healed. I caught myself feeling sorry for Joynes. I quickly put the pity away. I knew he wouldn't want it.

The nurse dabbed at the red hole with the cotton.

"Maybe you could come talk to me more often," Joynes said to the nurse. He winked at her. "Sure improves the view." The nurse smiled and kept on dabbing. Joynes winced and groaned each time the peroxide hit the wound. I could only imagine the pain; I winced along with him. But he kept right on talking, flirting with the nurse. The guy was tough.

"I know this hurts, Sergeant," she said. "You don't have to be brave."

Joynes gave her a crooked grin. "Hurts so good, honey. Keep it coming. I gotta get back to my platoon. They're counting on me."

She smiled again and shook her head.

A couple of weeks later I pulled prisoner patrol at the 67th again. Joynes was gone, sent back to "the world," they told me. I was happy for him, but I wondered what he'd be doing in a year or two with a giant hole in his body.

Walking the back row, the faces had changed, but the damage hadn't. GIs like me lying there with no hands, or feet sheared off, or bodies shredded from shrapnel and bullet wounds. Ripped apart in all sorts of horrible ways. Nurses came in every now and again and changed their dressings and they'd moan or shout out.

PFC Goodridge, a lanky black guy with massive lower-leg injuries was now in Joynes's bed. Fluids of every color ran in and out of him through a complicated tangle of tubes. He woke up the last few minutes of my shift and, like Joynes, seemed grateful for some company.

"Punji sticks," he rasped. "You ever heard of those?"

I shook my head. "Some kind of booby trap?"

"Bamboo stakes," Goodridge explained, "sharpened up like skewers. Congs stick those mothers point side up in the ground, camouflage 'em with the brush."

His brows lowered. "Punjis, see, they ain't meant to kill right off the bat." His voice turned hard. "Just cripple." He paused for a moment, grinding his teeth. I could see his temples pulse. Then he went on. "Congs coat the points with shit or poison, see. They just hoping a massive infection'll eat us up from the inside out."

I couldn't believe what I was hearing. Dirty, rotten tricks. That wasn't how you were supposed to fight a war.

I shook my head. "That's cold, man," I said. "Evil."

Goodridge nodded weakly. "It's a tactical thing, for the Congs. If the poor sucker who got stuck wants to keep his legs, see, medevac's got to get him out ASAP. And then you done given away your unit's position—plus handed Victor Charlie a big-money helo target." He coughed, a dry kind of hacking with a rattle deep inside. It didn't sound good. "And that's what happened out there, man. With me. We was running search and destroys up near An Khe. I got hit with the sticks and . . . I let 'em down, man, my brothers, I . . ."

He looked away.

All of a sudden I felt—well, I didn't know what I felt. I didn't know anything.

I felt helpless, out of control. Like treading water, when your legs and arms are moving, but you're really not going anywhere.

I didn't know why we were here, Goodridge and Joynes and me and everybody else. I didn't know about this war, all the hows and whys. They'd told us the North Vietnamese, the Congs, wanted Communism, and the South Vietnamese wanted democracy. And something about if all of Vietnam went Communist, well, it would be the beginning of the end for the free world. Like dominoes—once one falls, it's all done.

I didn't know what kind of life guys like Joynes and Goodridge and all the rest of the wounded Americans lying in hospitals across Vietnam could look forward to. I didn't know what in the hell was worth that kind of sacrifice. Bringing truth, justice, and the American Way to the Ree-public of Vietnam? Domino theories? I didn't know why the Vietnamese were so goddamned important, more important than American kids. Ten years ago nobody'd ever even heard of this place.

And I didn't know how I ever got it so lucky. I didn't know why I slept in a tent, soon to be barracks, instead of a muddy foxhole. Why I downed three hot squares in a mess hall rather than cold beef stew out of a C-rat can. Tooled around in a jeep all day rather than humped ammo through the jungle, Charlie behind every tree waiting to blow me up or stake my legs with poison.

I didn't know why my Vietnam War was miles apart from their Vietnam War.

My chest felt tight. I took a deep breath and tried to think of something bright, something hopeful, something . . . cheery . . . to say. All I could come up with was, "Well, hey, you got yourself a ticket back home."

Goodridge gave a sad little laugh and closed his eyes. "But I just got here, man."

We stayed quiet.

"So where is home?" I asked, trying to change the subject.

He kept his eyes closed. "Detroit," he said flatly.

"We got a guy in our company from Detroit," I said,

thinking of Wright. "He's okay. Detroit must be a cool place to live."

"Motor City," Goodridge said, eyes still shut. "Motown, man."

"Home of the Supremes," I said. "You dig 'Baby Love'?"

His eyes flew open. "You know the Supremes?"

"Of course," I said. "Diana Ross—voice of an angel."

"Not to mention one foxy lady," Goodridge said. I thought I saw a glimmer of a twinkle in his eye.

"And the Temptations," I said, "don't forget them." I sang a line of "My Girl." "Now that's some righteous songwriting. And those harmonies—nobody can touch those guys."

Goodridge gave me a long, hard stare. Then he flashed a huge grin.

"You know the Four Tops?" he asked.

I pulled out my nightstick and sang "I Can't Help Myself" into it like a microphone.

Goodridge chuckled. "How about Stevie Wonder?"

I whipped out my sunglasses, slid them on, and belted out the chorus to "Uptight (Everything's Alright)."

Goodridge laughed so hard he started to cough, then cry.

"How you know so much about music, MP?" he said, wiping away the tears and struggling to catch his breath.

"I was in a band back home," I told him.

"Yeah?" he said, like he knew it all along. "I bet you was the singer."

"And guitar."

"Your band play Motown?"

I shoved the nightstick back into my belt. "Nah, we were more into the British Invasion stuff. The Beatles—"

"Oh, man, I love me some Beatles."

My brows rose over my sunglasses. "You do?"

"What, a Motor City brother can't dig himself some 'Twist and Shout'? Some 'Help'? Some 'Eleanor Rigby'?"

"You've got good taste." I smiled.

He pointed to my glasses. "Gimme those." I handed them to him. He put them on and said in his best John Lennon accent, "We're bigger than Jesus, you know."

I cracked up.

"What else your band play?" he asked, handing back the glasses.

"Some Stones, some Kinks, some Dave Clark Five. We did our own stuff too."

"You write songs?"

I slid the sunglasses back into my shirt pocket. "Yeah. I wrote a couple for the band. We got 'em down on tape, if you can believe it. Found a recording studio near our town that would work with teenagers."

Goodridge looked at me thoughtfully. "You want to do music when you get back to "the world," MP? Make a big record and get on the radio or something?"

It slipped out before I could stop it.

"Actually, we had a record deal before I left. Got the

contract and my draft notice the same week." The words tasted sour in my mouth.

"No lie?" Goodridge shook his head. "Now what's the odds of that happening? So how your band get a record deal?"

"My uncle Roy. He was our manager. Took that tape we made up to New York City."

Goodridge thought for a moment. "Can't you make your record after you get back?"

I looked at my boots. They were covered in a film of red dust. "No, man—record company didn't want to wait," I said. I tried to laugh, but it got caught in my throat. "I guess they weren't sure I'd be coming back."

Goodridge was quiet.

"You love music, don't you, MP?"

I nodded.

"Then you know that's what you gotta do when you get back. You gotta get yourself another record deal. You gotta make a record. That's what you gots to do." He grabbed my arm and pulled me close. He looked straight into my eyes. "You listen to me, MP. I can tell you got a heart for this music thing. I can see it. You a musician, not a killer."

His words sounded good in my ears, and something heavy lifted from my shoulders as he let go of my arm.

Halloran stuck his head in the door. "Hey, Kohler, shift's over. We're all headin' to the jeep."

I told him I'd be right there.

73

I stuck my hand out and Goodridge grabbed it.

"Thanks, man," I said. "You get yourself healed up, okay?"

He put his other hand on top of mine. "You come back and talk to me," he said. "You sing me some more songs."

As I walked out the door, Goodridge called out, "You okay, MP. You okay."

10

LEADBETTER'S REQUEST

I was sitting on my cot, tipping my boots upside down, giving them a few good whacks. Spiders, as usual. Huge, hairy, ugly. They tumbled to the wood-pallet floor and scuttled off like overweight crabs. One month in-country and I still wasn't used to the monster bugs here, like mutant insects from another planet.

"Private Kohler, just the man I'm looking for."

Leadbetter. He grinned and gave me a friendly thump on the back.

"Captain?" I said, standing up and saluting.

"Instruments," he said, returning my salute. He fished his pipe and lighter from his pocket. "We gotta find you guys some instruments."

Instruments? *He can't be for real.*

"You serious, sir?" I asked him.

"Damn straight, Private," he said, snapping his Zippo

shut, a halo of vanilla smoke rising to the tent top. "The new barracks are going in. We got the mess up. The Longbranch is finished. What we need now is some music. What the hell's a bar without a band? A bar's got to have a band."

"Yes, sir. Entertainment. Good idea."

Leadbetter wiped the sweat from his forehead and the back of his thick neck. "I don't care how you do it or how long it takes. Can I count on you to make it happen, Kohler?"

A rock band? In Nam? *Not damn likely.*

"Of course, sir," I told him. "You can count on me."

I thought about Captain's request—command, really—all day long. I was on prisoner patrol again, this time at the hospital out in the Valley, next to the MP battalion head-quarters. It was a good thing it was at HQ, too. The VC prisoners there were injured, but they could get up and walk around. They put five of us on at a time. We kept a guard station at each corner of the ward, where we stood with 12-gauge sawed-off shotguns. We weren't messing around. Then one of us, unarmed, stayed inside with the prisoners.

It was my lucky day.

The Congs spent their time sitting, sleeping, or hanging out in groups of three or four. Talked to one another in Vietnamese. We couldn't understand them. And they never looked us in the eye. Their faces were always blank. Probably talking about us, maybe even plotting against us.

It always made me nervous. That's why I liked the outside guard positions with the shotgun best.

Today, though, the prisoners were quiet. Yesterday, four of them went over the fence. The land was pretty open out there in the Valley, but then it blended right into rice paddies and farmers' fields, rows of green upon green and darker green. Guess they thought if they could get over that fence and out to one of those paddies, they might have a fighting chance. Big negative on that idea. Our guys were on the radio in a flash. A helicopter swooped down in seconds, machine guns blasting. Driscoll said the runaways jerked around for an instant, then vanished into red mist.

Watching the Congs share their secrets, I rolled Captain's idea over and over in my mind. There were so many reasons why it wouldn't work, why it couldn't work. I wondered why I had even agreed to it in the first place. No instruments. No equipment. And that was just for starters. Where would a band practice, in a sandbag bunker? And, sure, we couldn't hide Dodge City from Charlie—it was a safe bet he already knew we were there—but did we really need to advertise our exact location with music?

I was starting to think that maybe Leadbetter was nuts. That I'd made a mistake. Maybe I should tell him it just couldn't be done.

Still, putting together another band . . . I couldn't get it out of my mind.

After the shift, on the way back to Dodge City, I

had Wright swing out by the airport, to the 67th EVAC hospital.

"What do you need here?" he asked as we pulled up. "You leave something last time?"

"Just wait for me," I told him. I hopped out of the jeep.

"Hurry up, man," he called after me. "This boy needs some chow."

Dersheimer and Voina were standing guard outside the VC ward.

"What are you doing here?" Dersheimer asked.

"Don't worry, no problems," I said, rushing past him.

I walked inside, looking for Goodridge.

I sucked in my breath. His eyes were closed. His face was sunken and ashy.

His legs were gone.

Goodridge opened his eyes.

A weak smile flickered on his cracked lips.

"MP," he whispered. He slid a fragile hand out from under the blanket. I took it.

"Hey, man." I didn't know what else to say. I didn't even know why I was there.

"Sing to me," Goodridge croaked. He shut his eyes.

My chest felt heavy. I moved closer and leaned over his bed. My face was near his ear.

Fighting to keep my voice steady, I sang the first verse from "Reach Out (I'll Be There)," then the chorus.

Goodridge ran out the tip of his tongue and tried to lick

his lips. His eyes were still closed. "Four Tops," he managed to whisper. He gave my hand a barely perceptible squeeze.

I stood there, silent, holding his hand, until I heard his breathing, shallow but steady, and I knew he was asleep.

Wright talked the whole ride back to Dodge City. I didn't hear a word.

It was a rare evening. So far, no ambushes. Just the nightly fireworks show, courtesy of tracers from Viet Cong gunfire high above our tents.

"You joking?" Sugden laughed, almost dropping the flashlight he was using to read in his rack.

"Hey, pipe down, we're trying to get some shut-eye here!" somebody yelled out.

"Captain's for real," I whispered, trying to get comfortable in my cot, the sheets damp as always. "He wants us to play again, like back at Bragg. Only here."

"Who?" Sugden whispered back. "You and Ioli and Voina?"

"I guess." I thought for a moment. "Ioli can handle it, I think."

"You could ask him in the morning. He's got the four to midnight tonight. What about Voina?"

"I don't know, man. I want to play stuff that's on the radio, new stuff. He likes the old stuff." I waved away a cloud of giant mosquitoes. "Besides, if I'm on guitar and Ioli's on drums, what we'd really need is a bass player. So what do you think?" I whispered. "You up for it?"

"What? Hell, yeah!" he said.

"Hey, shut it up over there!" somebody else yelled.

Sugden lowered his voice. "But where the hell are we going to find instruments in this dump? Black market?"

"No idea," I said, reaching for my pocket calendar and pen on the footlocker next to my cot. I squinted in the dark and crossed out another day. "I just told Captain I'd do it."

"Even if we could find some, how we gonna pay for them? We ain't got that kind of cash." Sugden pulled off his glasses and rubbed his eyes.

"I don't know," I said, using the point of my pen to silently count off my time left. Three hundred and six days to go.

"Sleep on it," he grunted, snapping off the flashlight. He rolled over. Soon he was snoring.

The rumble of distant artillery rattled my cot. I didn't think I'd ever get used to it.

I lay on my back. I thought about the old farmer in the paddy. The kid hanging upside down at the PX. Mom. VC in the mud. The Satellites' last gig. Goodridge. Leadbetter asking if he could count on me. Roy.

Roy. Damn, I missed him.

What would Roy do? I wondered.

Roy was good at making things happen. Like the Satellites' record deal.

Roy liked our songs from the recording studio so much

that he took the acetate, our demo record, up to New York City. Just walked in the door at Capitol Records like he was some hotshot manager, told the folks there that he had a record they needed to hear.

Roy was relentless. Mom could tell you. He was her baby brother, but he was like an older brother to me; we were only twelve years apart. Roy was the type of guy that you know isn't going to go away, so you go ahead and listen to him just to get him out of there. And that's exactly what happened at Capitol. He got a "thanks, but no thanks" and was politely shown the door.

But Roy was no quitter. He got on the elevator with a lady from Tower Records, a subsidiary of Capitol. By the time the doors opened again, he'd locked up the Satellites' record deal.

I still couldn't believe it. Somebody thought my music was good. Good enough to put on a record for the whole world to hear.

Definitely not Dad. I wished he could be more like Roy. Wished he knew what it felt like to be up on a stage, making a groove, sharing your music. But Dad just didn't get it.

So Roy came home from New York with the record deal.

I showed him the draft notice. It had come just four weeks after my nineteenth birthday. The Satellites' golden opportunity, gone in an instant.

But Roy had made things happen.

And so will I.

Moonlight filtered through the tent flap. I pulled a piece of USO stationery from my pack.

Dear Gretsch Guitar Company,

We are soldiers of the United States Army 127th Military Police Company based in Qui Nhon, Vietnam. A few of us play music, but we have no place to buy things. There are no stores around here that sell American musical equipment. We were wondering if we could buy directly from you? We would appreciate it if you would please let us know as soon as you can. Music would really help morale here. Thank you very much.

Sincerely,
PVT Dean Kohler
U.S. Army

MUSIC ON MY MIND

The next day, McClory found me in the mess hall at lunchtime. He looked serious.

"Your friend at the EVAC hospital." He shook his head. "Just before midnight. Sorry, man." He walked away and left me with my chow.

So that was it? Gone. Just like that.

I stared at my peas for a long time.

That night I had gate guard duty at the MP station downtown, the four-to-midnight shift. It was my least-favorite duty, sitting in the shack at the front entrance with a waist-high wall of sandbags in front. Once the downtown patrol jeeps were gone, there was nothing much to do. Boring, with a capital B. Tonight, though, I didn't mind it. I was craving the solitude.

I thought about Goodridge and how he felt he'd failed his unit. I thought about the Motown music he'd loved so much and his John Lennon impersonation. I smiled. He'd called me a musician, not a killer. I wondered if he was in a better place, where kids didn't run around in jungles carrying guns.

My chest ached. I tried to shove my thoughts away.

I rested my chin on my hands and gazed across the driveway. The restaurant next door was closed up for the night, though the smell of cooking grease still hung in the humid air. I had eaten there a couple of times. Soon as you sat at the counter, the papasan would come over and say, "Hom and chee, Coke? Hom and chee, Coke?" The sandwich was some kind of canned processed-ham product and a square of bland cheese. Pretty tasteless. The Cokes were bottled somewhere in Vietnam, with barely any carbonation. These days, I stuck with the mess hall and the snack bar at the PX. Semi-passable burgers and dogs, canned Cokes, and you didn't have to worry that the burger'd been pulling the plow the day before.

The restaurant was dark, but through the open door of a small balcony, I noticed the blue, flickering light of a TV set. The only channel to tune in to at this hour was Armed Forces Television, courtesy of Uncle Sam.

I leaned out the guard shack window. If I scrunched my eyelids the right way, I could just make out the glimmering picture on the tiny screen. I could hear the TV announcer, very faint, "Coming up next, the Beatles, live at Shea Stadium!"

Papasan treated me to a full hour of the Fab Four.

This one's for you, Goodridge.

"Face it, Dean, we just ain't got the dough." Ioli rammed a wire brush down the barrel of his M14.

Sugden, Ioli, and I were sitting on the tent floor. Cleaning rods, brushes, and tubes of LSA were strewn across the pallets as we worked on our weapons.

Sugden and I had told Ioli about Captain's band idea. He'd laughed his butt off at first—until he saw we were serious. Then he was in too. But now it sounded like he wanted out.

"What, you don't want to do the band?" I asked him.

He shoved the brush back and forth. "No, man, that ain't what I'm saying at all. All's I know is that we're E-3s, almost the bottom of the totem pole. And two hundred bucks a month don't stretch too far, you know?"

"Especially if you're sending most of it back home to the old lady," Sugden said. A cigarette hung from his mouth as he wiped down his rifle. "Doesn't leave much pocket change."

I chucked my rag at him. "So what else is new? I've been buying your burgers since MP school. Smokes too. So, what, you're backing out now too?"

"Dean, we just ain't got the cash to buy all the stuff we're gonna need," Ioli said.

Sugden backed him up. "Besides the instruments—if we

can even find them somewhere—there's gonna be amps, a PA system—"

"Sticks and strings," Ioli added. "You really think we're gonna find all that here?"

I didn't need to hear all the reasons why a band wouldn't work. I'd gone over them a million times in my own head over the last week.

I didn't say anything. I carried my cleaned and oiled M14 over to the rifle rack and locked it up next to the others.

"Look, you know we're with you, man," Sugden said. "A band, here—nothing would be cooler. But you gotta realize that maybe it's not realistic. Maybe it's not feasible. Maybe Captain's asking for the impossible, you know?"

I knew they were right. But now I was even more determined to make the band happen.

"Yeah, well, we'll see," I said.

That night, I wrote three more letters. One each to the Fender and Gibson guitar companies, and one to Shure, the microphone makers.

If we could scrape together enough money, if we could buy what we needed from them . . . maybe . . .

A START

Two days later, they teamed me with the FNG, Klazinski, from Four Squad. I'd been in Qui Nhon two months, though it felt like two years. Klazinski had been in-country four days. He was tall and thin, pimple-faced and petrified. He barely said a word as we took off into town.

Back in August, the rest of us had all been sent from MP school at Fort Gordon to Fort Bragg in North Carolina to form the new MP company, the 127th. Since we hadn't been scheduled to ship out until December, they'd needed to find something for us to do—like training. And more training. And more training. Assault training. Jungle training. Advanced weapons training. We were proficient with M60 machine guns, the M79 grenade launcher, the 3.5 rocket launcher, the M14 and M16 rifles, the .45 caliber pistol. When we weren't training, we patrolled with the MP company stationed at Bragg. In other words, we knew our stuff.

Klazinski, he was fresh out of MP school. Never even been on a patrol before.

The shift started out quietly. The briefing at the MP station downtown was routine. The streets were congested, as usual, but traffic was moving despite the misty March rain. It was still too early in the morning for the bar crowd, and the ARVN stationed on the street corners, rifles at the ready, seemed to be keeping the locals in line.

Klazinski sat in the passenger seat, his fingers kneading the flak jacket in his lap. Rivulets of sweat trickled from under his MP helmet. I wondered if I'd looked that pathetic when I first got here. I sort of felt sorry for him. But something about him made me angry, too. I wanted to shake him and shout, "You're in Vietnam, dude. Get a goddamn grip." But I kept silent.

As we started our third circle around downtown, he lit up a cigarette. I could see the lighter tremble in his hand. "H-how is it here?" he asked softly. He'd been so quiet, it startled me to hear him speak.

"Not too bad," I said. "You just have to keep your eyes open and—"

The police radio crackled. Possible VC down at the PT boat piers.

I yanked the steering wheel, squealed into a U-turn, and tore off for the causeway out to the piers.

Klazinski sunk low in his seat. "Bad . . . bad . . . this is bad," he started muttering, over and over.

And this is my backup. Terrific.

Within two minutes, we'd screeched up to the guard gate at the piers. There was a single guard, all alone, and he looked very happy to see us.

Fastening my flak jacket, I jumped out of the jeep and surveyed the sandy open field behind the guard gate. Beyond the field, I could see a fleet of World War II PT boats tied up at the dock, their wooden hulls glistening in the drizzle.

The guard, a chunky kid with glasses, jogged out to meet me.

"What happened?" I asked him.

"I saw somebody down by the boats," he panted. "Looked like he was messing around with 'em or something. He was all in black. I'd go down there, but I can't leave my post. I'm the only one here."

I nodded and turned, thinking Klazinski was at my side. He was still in the jeep.

For crying out loud.

"Hey, Klazinski, let's go!" I barked.

He looked like a man on the way to the firing squad as he got out of the jeep, his face screwed up tight, every move slow and deliberate.

"Draw your pistol and stay alert," I told him as we walked across the sandy field. I scanned in every direction but didn't see anyone.

"Now we're going to check between the boats," I told

Klazinski when we reached the wooden pier. His gun quivered in his hand. I wondered if maybe it would be better if he were unarmed.

Everything was still. All we could hear was the slap of water on wood. Our search between the boats turned up nothing.

"M-maybe there's no one here," Klazinski said. "M-maybe we should go now."

"Quiet," I said. "We're going to have to look boat by boat."

I noticed that one boat was docked by itself, while the rest were all together. I moved to the stand-alone and hopped over onto the deck. Klazinski followed about twenty steps behind me.

A hatch in the boat's deck—square, metal—caught my attention. Without a word, I motioned Klazinski over and pointed my .45 at the hatch. I gestured for him to aim too. He held his gun with both trembling hands, eyes big as canteens.

My heart pounded against my ribs as I slowly reached down. I held my breath, then flipped open the door.

Nothing. Just a black hole. I exhaled. I wanted to look into the hole, but I sure as hell wasn't going to stick my head in there.

Then Klazinski cocked his gun. He clutched it, shaking, over the hatch.

I couldn't believe it. Maybe he thought he was going to

be a hero or something. "What the hell are you doing?" I whispered.

"W-what do you think? I'm gonna fire a couple of shots down in there," he said, his soft voice rising, high and panicky.

Brilliant.

"The boat's made of wood," I reminded him. "You're not shooting any holes in the bottom of this boat. It'll sink."

Klazinski gave me an "oh" look and lowered his weapon.

I didn't know why, but at that moment an episode of my favorite TV show back home flashed in my mind. "I have a better idea," I said in a low voice.

I left the hatch open and we stepped off the boat back onto the pier.

"Get in the jeep," I whispered in Klazinski's ear. "Rev it a few times, make it obvious you're fixing to leave. Then drive up to the gate. When you get there, sit with the guard and watch me. If you see anything that's not looking cool, come back and help me out."

"O-okay," he mumbled. He looked like remembering my instructions was giving him a migraine.

As Klazinski clomped off down the pier, I crept back up onto the boat, hoping his footsteps were masking mine. I squatted down beside the hatch.

Klazinski got in the jeep. He started it up, revved it a few times, then headed for the gate. The sound of the motor faded off into the distance.

I sat there in the gray rain, .45 in my hand. Waiting. Stone. Not a muscle twitching, barely breathing. Eyes wide, welded to the hatch.

All of a sudden a head popped up.

Gotcha.

I shoved my pistol into his neck. He froze.

"Dung lai!"—stop!—I yelled, my throat tight. It was weird. I should have been scared out of my wits. But I wasn't. I expected him, but I didn't. I felt excited, my heart racing in my ears.

I lifted the little man out of the hatch, gun barrel at his head. He had on the black silk pajamas, the straw hat in his hand. I walked him to the end of the pier, my gun in his back, and signaled Klazinski. And signaled him again. And signaled him once more.

Jesus.

Finally, he drove up to the pier. He jumped out, acting nervous and goofy.

"H-how'd you know, how'd you know?" he asked, eyes bulging, skinny arms flailing.

"Guess you never saw that episode of *The Andy Griffith Show*," I said as I searched the guy.

He had a piece of black silk folded up in his waistband. In it was a little bit of money, a knife, and a U.S. Navy issue cigarette lighter.

Was he going to set the boats on fire? Ambush the guard?

As usual, there was no way to tell.

We handcuffed him and took him in to the MP station.

1630 hours. Mail call. Klazinski and I had just come in from patrol. He was still wigged out from his first VC encounter. He'd chain-smoked all the way back to Dodge City.

And there it was. An envelope from Shure.

> *Dear Private Kohler,*
>
> *We are in receipt of your letter and are happy to inform you that you may purchase Shure products directly from us.*
>
> *It is our pleasure to extend to you a military discount on our Unidyne 55 microphones, which normally retail for $100 each. Your price is $30 each.*
>
> *We look forward to serving your musical needs. Good luck to you and your company.*
>
> *Sincerely,*
> *Shure Brothers Incorporated*
> *Microphones and Acoustic Devices*

I found Sugden and Ioli at the Longbranch. There were a few other guys sitting around, drinking beers and playing cards. I got a Coke from the bartender and walked over to Sugden and Ioli's table.

I stood there grinning at them, feeling like I was about to burst.

Sugden grabbed my arm and yanked me into a seat. "Spill it, Kohler."

I handed the letter to Ioli. "Check it out."

"No freakin' way!" Ioli hollered, hopping up from his chair. He did a little dance around the table, his beer held high over his head. The other guys shrugged, then went back to their cards.

Sugden pushed up his glasses and read the letter. "Kohler, you sly bum. I can't believe it. You did it—you found us some mikes."

I felt like getting up and dancing, too, but I kept myself under control. "It's a start, anyway."

"A beauteous start," Ioli said, dropping back into his seat.

Sugden's wheels were already turning. "Now, if we could get a guitar company to do the same thing . . ." He lit up a cigarette.

"I'm way ahead of you, man," I said. "I wrote to Fender, Gretsch, and Gibson weeks ago." I pointed to the letter on the table. "Looks like we need to order ourselves some microphones."

GUITARS

A letter from Judy and the package from Shure arrived the same day. I didn't know which to open first.

I tore open the pink envelope.

March 14, 1967

Dear Dean,

How are you? School is keeping me pretty busy this semester, especially Mrs. Conashek and algebra.

I've been chosen to represent my class for the Miss Cradock competition. I'm still figuring out what I'll do for the talent part of it, maybe play the piano. Wish me luck!

Everybody says hi—

Judy

Okay. So it was a nice letter. Friendly, and nice. Nothing lovey-dovey or anything. Why would it have been? We'd left it open-ended, right? The letter was just—nice. I was living in the mud and dodging the enemy, and Judy was doing algebra and worrying about a beauty pageant.

I shoved the letter into my pocket and walked into the tent.

Jessen and Sanchez from One Squad were hanging out with Sugden and Ioli. They were talking about Suttle, who'd apparently brought a portable turntable with him to Nam. My ears pricked up at the conversation.

"And his wife sends him all the latest records, man," Jessen was saying excitedly from his seat on an empty ammo crate.

Sugden looked up from his paperback. "Who brings a record player to Vietnam?"

"We didn't even know he had the thing until mail call yesterday," Jessen said. "Suttle gets this package and it's four record albums. The new ones from Donovan and the Byrds, and some other bands I never heard of."

"Grateful Dead," Sanchez pitched in.

"Boss name for a band," I said.

"So Suttle brings out this leather box with a handle on it," Jessen went on, "and we all think it's a mini-suitcase or something. He plugs this thing in and slaps on a record. Bingo! We've got music." He noticed the big black logo on the package in my hands.

"Shure?" Jessen said. "What's that?"

Sugden and Ioli almost knocked the other guys over scrambling to the crate.

"What?" Jessen said, bewildered. "What is it?"

We stood around the box, staring at it like it was the Holy Grail.

Slowly, carefully, I slid my penknife under the box flaps, slicing through the brown paper tape.

And there they were, three gleaming microphones.

"Hoo-*eee*! Would you take a look at those?" Ioli yelped. He reached in and picked one up, turning it back and forth like a jewel under the tent's bare lightbulb. Sugden and I grabbed the other two.

Sugden whistled. "Top of the line, baby."

I ran my fingers over the smooth metal. The mike felt heavy, solid, in my hands. Just like I remembered, leaning out over the stage at the Satellites' shows, girls squealing, guys cheering.

"Nice." I was pumped.

"Microphones?" Jessen puzzled. "Wait a minute, are you guys putting together a band?"

Sugden, Ioli, and I grinned at one another.

Jessen pointed an accusatory finger at the three of us. "You *are* doing a band, aren't you?"

Ioli held his mike up to his mouth and took a bow. "Thank you, thank you very much," he said, Elvis-style.

Sugden placed his mike carefully back in the box. "So

nothing from the guitar companies?" he asked me.

I shook my head.

"Man, we shoulda heard somethin' by now, right?" Ioli handed me his mike and I put it in the box with the others.

Sugden lit up a cigarette. "Well," he said, "if we want to do an a cappella vocal thing, we're all set."

Sugden and I were cutting through town from prisoner patrol out in the Valley. Past the paddies and the sugarcane. Past the graveyards and tangled hedgerows. The beer-can hovels with shoeless babysans playing in the muck. Into the chaos of downtown.

Then we spotted them. I almost wrecked the jeep. We couldn't believe our eyes.

Guitars. Amps, too. Even drums.

They were sitting in one of those open-air general stores. Maybe they were garbage. Maybe not. But they were musical instruments, and we were psyched. We hopped out to take a look.

I picked up a guitar, gleaming black with a red pick guard. I flipped it over. MADE IN FRANCE was stamped on the back. Even so, it was as close to an American-built Fender Stratocaster as you could possibly get. I tested it.

"Any good?" Sugden asked, cigarette dangling from the side of his mouth.

"Doesn't play so bad," I said. I was surprised.

I had a '63 Gretsch Tennessean back home, a real beauty. I'd always thought of a Strat as a guitar for surf guys like the Beach Boys and Dick Dale. My gorgeous Gretsch cost me $415 in Satellites gig money. It was glad it was tucked safely under my bed at home.

"Doesn't touch a Gretsch," I said. "But it's not bad."

Standing there with a guitar in my hands again, I felt different. Like myself, but not myself. Like someone I used to know a long, long time ago.

Sugden picked up what resembled a Fender Jazz bass. Nam-made, he told me. Sunburst. It didn't look like the best quality, but it definitely seemed workable.

"How's it feel?" I asked.

"Good," he said, snapping and popping the bottom strings. "It's okay. Better than I thought."

We plugged the guitars into a couple of amplifiers set up nearby. From a distance, the amps looked almost like Fender Bassman or Tremolux units, popular back home. When we got up close, though, it was obvious they were knockoffs. The knobs weren't exactly right, the faceplates were a little off.

Close enough.

I gave the Strat-alike a strum, then picked and noodled on it a bit. Sugden plucked out a rhythm on the bass. The guitars didn't sound too bad through the knock-off amps. I wondered how they'd sound through my Fender Showman amp back home.

In a minute, Papasan was all over us. "Good price for good GIs! Good price for good GIs!"

We'd been saving for weeks, thinking the guitar companies were going to come through. But we had guitars in our hands—right here and now—and they were okay. Not great. But definitely okay.

Sugden looked over at me, eyebrows raised. I gave him a discreet nod, then turned to Papasan. "How much?" I asked.

After about ten minutes of haggling, we finally talked him down to $125 for my guitar, $100 for Sugden's, and $125 apiece for the amps. A bargain, considering a Strat back home would run around $300, same with a Jazz bass, and a Bassman amp would set you back $350.

Papasan counted our dough behind the counter.

"All right, man," Sugden said. "Mikes, guitars, amps. It's getting closer."

"I don't know," I said, wondering if we should've waited to hear from the guitar companies. "I'm not sure this gear's going to be good enough to pull it off."

Sugden shook his head and lit up another smoke. "Ease up, Dean. We're in a war zone. We live in the mud. It's the best we can do."

I supposed he was right.

We loaded the jeep and headed for Dodge City.

Ioli about flipped his lid when we rolled up.

"*Beee*-utiful!" he said. He stroked the top of an amp and

fiddled with the knobs. "Oh, baby, we are gonna do this! Where'd you get all this stuff?"

"Downtown," Sugden said, pulling out the bass. "We were riding back from the Valley and saw it all out there, in one of them papasan shops."

"No lie?" Ioli said. "Beautiful!"

"Yeah, man." I grabbed the Stratocaster. "And they've got drums too."

"Right *on!*" Ioli grinned and did an air snare roll and cymbal crash.

Some of the other guys from the company crowded around to get a look.

"Hey, does Leadbetter know?" Jim Leach asked in his Indiana farmer-boy twang. He was the only guy I knew who actually dropped out of high school to join up. He lifted an amp from the jeep for us.

"Not yet," said Sugden, gathering guitar cords from under the seat.

A nasal whine broke in. "He ain't gonna let you boys keep that stuff."

Lupica. Voina's buddy. We should've known. Ever since the guys knew that we were trying to put a band together, he'd been working a bad attitude. Glaring at us in the mess hall, making stupid remarks in the Longbranch, like, "Watch out, rock stars on the loose!" We'd just ignored him. I figured he was pissed because we hadn't asked Voina, with his Strat, to join. Lupica probably thought that since his friend Voina had done that last hurrah thing with us at Bragg he was entitled to instant membership.

I liked Voina, but I couldn't understand how he could hang around with a moron like Lupica. And I didn't need Lupica's bull, not today. He could start his own damn band.

Sugden, who stood a head taller and about twenty pounds heavier, got in Lupica's face. "What's your problem, man?" Sugden growled.

Lupica put his hands up in the air and backed away. "Just lettin' you know that Captain ain't gonna let you keep all that rock-star equipment. I'm just sayin'."

"We'll see about that," I said, handing the Strat-alike to Ioli and grabbing the other amp from the jeep.

Sugden gave Lupica a sidelong scowl. "Let's go," said Sugden, and we headed for the tent.

Inside, I cracked open my amp to take a look at the guts.

It was force of habit. When I was a kid, I was always taking things apart and putting them back together again, like Roy's reel-to-reel recorder, just to see how stuff worked.

Everyone crowded around as I unscrewed the back off the speaker cabinet. We burst out laughing. It looked like a kid's toy inside.

Next, I slid the circuit-board tray—the inner workings of the amp—out of the box. There was almost nothing to it. But for some reason, the phony amp worked. I plugged in

the Strat and started playing. The sound was pretty clean—
I turned it up—and loud.

Loud enough to bring Leadbetter to our tent.

Captain strode through the flap, his barrel chest leading
the way.

He whipped off his sunglasses. "What you got there,
Private?"

Everyone scrambled to their feet and saluted.

Leadbetter returned our salute. "As you were," he said.

We all relaxed—a little.

"Instruments, sir," I said. "Sugden and I, we secured
some guitars and amplifiers in town today, sir."

Through the flap, I noticed Lupica and his buddies loi-
tering. Lupica was wearing a big smirk.

Captain knelt down to check out the amps. He twisted a
couple of knobs. Flipped the ON/OFF switches. Frowning, he
took the Strat-alike from me and gave it a strum.

My mind went back and forth. Leadbetter had asked me
to get the guitars. But who had ever heard of having a rock
band in the middle of a war? A big, fat audio bull's-eye for
the VC. No way the army condoned that. Maybe Captain
had changed his mind. Maybe this wasn't such a hot idea
after all.

Leadbetter handed the guitar back to me.

"So"—he grinned, pulling out his pipe—"when does
practice start?"

Practice? It took me a second to find my voice. "As

soon as possible, sir," I said, trying to quash a giant smile. I glanced outside. Lupica and his pals had disappeared.

"Excellent," Captain said, turning on his heel. "By the way, my favorite song's 'I Fought the Law.'" He returned our salute, then waved his pipe. "Carry on."

Ioli headed down to Papasan's the very next day. He came back the proud owner of a four-piece drum set: bass, snare, one mounted tom, one floor tom. They were all Nam-made, in kind of a cheesy yellow-brown finish.

"Man, these things are hid-*eee*-ous," Ioli said as Jessen and Sugden helped him lay them out on the pallet sidewalk.

"Why don't you paint 'em?" Jessen suggested.

We taped off the drum heads.

In minutes, Ioli's new Nam set was army-issue blue from a spray can.

THE FIRST PRACTICE

A few days later, Jessen and I were on patrol, weaving the jeep through a tangle of morning traffic on the outskirts of town. Vietnamese civilians rode rickshaws and motorbikes, women balanced bundles on their heads, toted babies on their hips. More people pushed carts full of chickens and ducks.

Navigating through the hubbub, I had to lay on the horn a few times.

"Sounds like your sax, Jessen." I laughed.

"Aw, I wasn't that bad," Jessen said, reaching over and thumping me on the head.

Back at Bragg, one weekend when most of the guys had gone into town on liberty, I'd heard a strange screeching, squawking sound. It seemed to be coming from the latrine. I walked in, and there was Jessen, honking on a saxophone.

"Hey, do you know how to play that thing?" I asked him

between squeaks and squonks. The answer was painfully obvious.

"Oh, nah, not really," he said, making a face. "Just bought it today." Jessen always seemed to have money. "I really play piano. Classical piano."

I wasn't sure I believed him. With his round face and red hair, Jessen looked more like a plump Howdy Doody than Liberace.

Now, on the road in Qui Nhon, I joked, "You know, your sax playing was so god-awful, I'm still not sure you were telling the truth about playing piano."

Jessen shrugged, then said, "Sounds like Sugden's getting pretty good." He'd been listening to Jon and me fooling around with the guitars back at Three Squad's tent. "You sure he never played bass before?"

"Yeah, he's coming along. He's got the easy stuff down, 'Louie, Louie' and 'Twist and Shout' and 'La Bamba.' Now we're working on the more complicated stuff. 'Mr. Tambourine Man' and a lot of the British songs."

"Yeah, I like that British sound."

"I'm teaching him some of the old standards, too. 'Rock Around the Clock,' 'Guitar Boogie Shuffle,' stuff with that rockabilly bass run. And some of the country tunes, 'Act Naturally,' 'Tiger by the Tail.' It would be great to hear them with drums, though. We're still looking for a good place to practice."

Jessen looked out at the paddies whizzing by. "You know

what song I used to really like back home?" he said. "It had this really boss keyboard line, the kind that gets stuck in your head, you know? I think it was called '96 Tears.'"

I nodded. "The Mysterians. Very cool song. Everybody likes that one."

And then it dawned on me. If we were going to do this band thing right, we were going to need a keyboard player. How could we do "96 Tears" without a keyboard?

All of a sudden, it seemed perfectly logical to ask Jessen to join. Maybe we could find a cheap keyboard at Papasan's or someplace. Even if Jessen couldn't play, well, no big deal, we'd still have the three of us, Sugden, Ioli, and me: bass, drums, and guitar.

"Hey, Ben," I said. "How would you feel about joining the band?"

He looked at me, eyes wide. He reminded me of a teddy bear. "Are you serious?"

I nodded. "We need a keyboard player, man."

Jessen beamed and gave me a double thumbs-up. "I'm in, buddy, I'm in!"

"Well, we're going to have to find you something to play first."

"No problem," Jessen said. "My folks, they'll go to Manny's Music and buy whatever I need. They'll ship it over."

Manny's Music, New York City. Uncle Roy had told me about it. Manny's was legendary, the primo-deluxe department store of musical equipment. Whatever you needed, anything you could possibly think of, they had it all right there, accordions to zithers.

"Must be nice," I said. "So maybe you're legit, after all." I chucked him on the bicep.

He tagged me back. "Thanks for the vote of confidence. So what do you think, what should I tell them to buy?"

I pondered for a moment, squinting into the sun as I drove. Then I told him, "Here's what you do. Ask them to get you a Farfisa Mini Compact organ." Jessen listened intently, nodding as I spoke. "It's the small version. It'll cost less than the big Farfisa, about four hundred and fifty instead of close to a grand. And it's lighter, should have a better chance of surviving the shipping . . ."

I didn't know how he did it, but the Farfisa Mini Compact organ arrived eight days later.

13 April, 1967

Dear Mom,

Thanks for the last care package, the puddings in the can are my favorite. I'm doing fine, patrols are okay. The days are still really hot, even the cool ones.

Could you do me a favor? Will you mail me my small amplifier? Roy can show you which one.

Dad probably won't be too happy to hear it, but we're putting together a little band over here. You can tell him it was our captain's idea, not

mine. Be sure to let Roy know too, I don't want
him to think I'm losing my guitar chops.

    Love to all back home,
    Dean
    P.S. Tell Mary to go easy on my car. And can
you send more Hit Paraders?

I folded up the letter, put it in an envelope, and sealed it up. I crossed out another day on my pocket calendar. One hundred twenty-four down, two hundred forty-one to go. I lay still in my rack. If this band thing worked, I hoped that time would fly.

Jake Sanino volunteered the supply tent for practice. Said he had plenty of space and just wanted to be around the music. Supply was located at the rear of our company area. The supply guys lived and worked out there. I guessed Jake was lonely more than he was a music lover, but I wasn't asking any questions.

The power generator that Leadbetter'd appropriated for our company was about a hundred feet or so behind supply, a little ways up the mountain. It made the perfect setup for us. We simply ran an extension cord from the generator to the back of supply and had plenty of juice for all the amps, plus the PA system I'd built from the amp Mom had sent.

And Captain Leadbetter was so happy we were ready to practice that he'd had the duty schedule reconfigured so we'd all be off at the same time.

We hauled the gear over to the supply tent. Guitars, amps, drums, cymbals, the organ, cables, cords, and microphones, including my old Satellites mike. Roy had made sure Mom sent it with my amp. Leach gave us a hand. He seemed as excited about the band as we were.

Finally, our first practice.

We started setting up, unpacking the microphones.

"Damn," said Sugden, pulling a Shure from the box. "No mike stands."

Guess we missed that little detail.

"We gotta have stands," Ioli said as he positioned a tom. "It's not like we can hold them things while we're playing."

I knelt over a tangle of cords. "Don't worry about it."

I didn't come this far to give up on account of some stupid mike stands.

"What, just don't use the mikes?" Jessen said.

"Give me a minute." I stood up and wiped the sweat from my forehead. "I'll think of something."

It was another sweltering day, one hundred degrees plus, even in the shade of the tent. I thought of the guys on the front lines, humping their packs in this heat. I hoped they were doing like Charlie, moving at night, digging in during the day. I stared outside at the mountain hooded in haze. Nearby, clumps of bamboo bent and swayed in the hot, sticky breeze. I got an idea.

I asked Sanino for a machete. He gave me the eagle eye for a second, then shrugged and handed over a giant knife. I gave it to Leach and sent him out into the scrub. He came back loaded with bamboo.

I asked the guys to help me pick through some lumber scraps behind the supply tent. We pulled out some plywood and two-by-fours. Sanino loaned me a hammer and nails. Within a few minutes, I'd put together a base. It was primitive but solid. I pulled out a bamboo stick—long, smooth, and straight—from Leach's pile and shoved it into the base. Then I attached my mike to the top.

The guys circled around my creation.

"Look at that," Jessen said approvingly.

Leach slapped his thigh. "Hot dang!"

"Beauteous!" said Ioli.

"You know, Mick Jagger wouldn't be caught dead with that," Sugden said, lighting up a smoke. He gave me a sideways smile. "Good job, man."

I put my hand around the mike and rocked the stand back and forth. It almost felt like the real thing. "Should get the job done."

"I'm making me one," Ioli said, and set off to search the tent. He came back with a wooden dowel, an empty coffee can, and a half-bag of cement.

Jessen took a scrap of rebar, the steel reinforcing rods we were using in the cement footings for the barracks, and hammered it into a four-by-four. He bent it on a slight curve, then attached the mike to it.

Jessen placed it proudly atop the Farfisa. "Presto! A gooseneck mike stand, army style."

"Whatever does the trick," I said, smiling at his creativity.

"Improvise, adapt, and overcome," Sugden said, putting the finishing touches on his own bamboo-and-plywood concoction. "The Marines would be proud of us lowly army schmucks."

We were ready.

"Let's do it," I said.

We plugged in the equipment and powered up. The amps crackled to life.

"*Yeee*-esssss!" Ioli pumped a drumstick.

He stomped double time on the bass drum pedal, churned out a snare roll, and finished with a cymbal crash, looking like the birthday boy who's just blown out the candles. I smiled back.

"Test, check, one, two, three," I enunciated into the mike, my voice blaring back at me from our makeshift PA speakers. I could hardly believe it—it was working.

"Oh, yeah, man!" Sugden chuckled as he warmed his fingers on the bass's lower strings, two inches of ash teetering at the end of the cigarette hanging from his mouth.

Jessen raked a hand across the Farfisa's keys and back; the warm, familiar organ tone filled the tent.

After a few minutes of limbering up, all faces turned to me.

Band practice. In Vietnam.

For a split second, I felt like I was going to cry. Then the bandleader in me took charge.

"All right, let's go!" I called out. "'Last Train to Clarksville.'"

Sugden and Ioli nodded, positioned themselves, waited for my cue.

Jessen's eyes looked like question marks.

"The Monkees?" I prodded.

Jessen's cheeks were flushed, his face blank. He shook his head. "Don't know it."

I wondered again if Jessen really knew how to play. I stifled a sigh.

"It's easy," I said. "Starts in G7, moves to C, back to G7. C again, then D. Then back to G7."

Jessen looked bewildered.

Now I was sure he didn't know how to play. Sugden looked down, pretending to tune his bass. Ioli fiddled with his snare. Leach shoved his hands in his pockets.

After a few moments, Jessen spoke. "You mean there are only three chords in the song?"

"Yes," I answered.

"Only three chords?" He scratched his head.

"Yes."

I'd never had to kick anyone out of a band before the first practice.

Jessen gave me a long, empty stare. He blinked. "You're

kidding, right?"

I tried to hide my irritation. "No, let me show you," I said, strumming a G7 as I walked over to the organ. I demonstrated the chord changes.

Jessen smiled when I was through.

"Man," he said, sounding hugely relieved. "I'm used to having thirteen or fourteen chords in the first four measures. All right, let's play!"

So I counted it off.

I knew I'd never have to worry about Jessen's musicianship again.

15

THE BANANA

"**O**kay, guys, let's do something easy," I said, giving the Strat-alike another warm-up strum. "McCoys. 'Hang on Sloopy.' In D." I turned to the Farfisa. "Ben, you got that?"

"Aye, aye, Captain," he said in his best pirate's brogue. We all rolled our eyes.

"That's Specialist, you smart-ass," I shot back playfully. Along with a handful of other guys in the company, I'd been promoted a few days before. E-3 to E-4, private to specialist. I knew Dad would be proud. Maybe I kind of was too.

I turned to Sugden, who was sitting on one of the supply guys' cots. "Sug, this'll be the boop-ba-boop-ba-boop sort of note hits."

He looked up at me like I'd just sprung a pop quiz. "You mean two notes for each chord change?"

I nodded. "Yep, just like that."

I looked over to the drum kit, set up between the cots.

"Mike, you do the intro by yourself, then the three of us will all come in together. You ready?"

Ioli nodded as if he knew exactly what I was talking about. But a second later he raised his sticks and said, "Hold it, hold it. What kind of drum intro?"

I fought back a sigh. This was starting to feel a lot like herding chickens. "It's like this, man." I tapped the rhythm on my microphone.

"Oh, yeah, yeah," Ioli said, waving a stick at me. "I remember that."

"Great," I said. "Then hit it."

Ioli launched the drum intro and Ben, Jon, and I came in behind him.

Something was off. Sugden's timing was wrong—he was getting behind.

"Whoa, whoa, hold it," I said into the mike. The song lurched to a stop. "Jon, man, you're a little slow on the notes."

Sugden rubbed at his hands like he was wringing wet laundry. "Geez, my fingers are sore. These strings are killers after a while."

I turned to the organ. "And Ben, could you make the chord changes a little smoother? They should flow."

He melted a few chords together.

"Exactly," I said, pleased that someone finally seemed to know what he was doing. I turned back to the drum set. "And Mike"—I couldn't resist—"since you're sitting so close to Sugden, he'd like some cheese to go with that whine."

Ioli and Jessen cracked up.

"Damned mouthy for a pipsqueak." Sugden snorted.

Ease up, Kohler, I told myself. Roy came to mind. He was always telling me to tone it down, not to expect perfection with the Satellites. That an audience never even notices mistakes.

Maybe I was expecting too much. I needed to turn these rookie players into a real band, and pissing them off probably wasn't the best idea. Still, if the whole thing didn't click along as a unit, it was going to make everybody look bad. I would look bad. I had to make this work.

"Okay," I said, adjusting my guitar strap. "From the top again."

The next run-through went better. It almost resembled a song. Out of the corner of my eye, I saw Leach and McClory creep into the tent.

"Sounding good," said Leach when we finished. McClory nodded. "The whole camp can hear it. Mind if we stick around?"

I looked at the band. We all shrugged. "Sure," I said. "Pull up a cot."

We did "Sloopy" a few more times. After the fifth go-round, it actually started sounding like the record. I could tell that everyone was really trying.

"Just like the radio," said Leach.

McClory nodded his agreement.

"Right on," said Ioli, twirling a drumstick. It danced

around his fingers, then skittered to the ground.

Everybody cracked up.

"Rock and roll!" he chirped, unfazed, as he picked it up.

"Here to stay." Ben hit the keys with a chord blast that made all of us jump. Ioli added a snare roll and cymbal crash.

"All right, you clowns," I said, smiling in spite of myself. "Back to work. 'Louie, Louie,' key of G."

The Youngbloods—Jesse Colin Young on vocals and bass, Jerry Corbitt on lead guitar, Joe Bauer on drums, and Lowell Levinger, who calls himself "Banana," on rhythm guitar—perhaps the tightest group in the country are nonetheless four very distinct musicians. You hear four separate things, but you feel one feeling. They are four quarters, working in perfect unity. . . .

I lowered the magazine and adjusted the pillow behind my head. The steel bunk, even with its thin mattress, beat a field cot in a GP-Medium any day. So did a roomy common area between the rows of bunks, with tables and chairs for playing cards, writing letters, holding chess tournaments. Now we even had a refrigerator to keep our cans of soda cold. All that was left of our old accommodations was the long pallet sidewalk that joined the new barracks to the shower.

The room was quiet, everyone reading or writing letters home or getting ready to turn in.

Four quarters, working in perfect unity.

That's what the guys and I had been working so hard to achieve the past few weeks. We spent most of our time over at supply now. When we weren't out on patrol, sleeping, or in the mess hall for chow, we were back at the supply tent, practicing. Leadbetter even had Jessen moved to Three Squad with the rest of us so the band could be together.

We knew about two sets' worth of material now, songs like "Under My Thumb" and "Satisfaction" by the Stones, "You Really Got Me" and "All Day and All of the Night" by the Kinks, "Wipe Out" by the Surfaris. Even a couple of my own songs I'd been working on after patrols. Before I shipped out, Uncle Roy had told me to keep writing. "The Satellites are going to need new songs when you get back," he said, locking me in a bear hug at my farewell family dinner.

The Satellites, Uncle Roy—it was all back in "the world." And worlds away.

Still, I was doing the best I could here. I'd shown the guys how the songs went, and they'd picked them all up pretty quickly. We were actually starting to sound like a real band. Like four quarters making a whole. Like what the Youngbloods article was saying.

We were moving in the right direction. Good enough that some of the guys would hike over to listen every once in a while. Giant, Sherman, McClory. One day, Leach

119

brought a tape recorder up to the tent, a small reel-to-reel he'd bought at the PX. He asked if he could record our practice. Now, we could listen to the playback and pick out where we were weak and needed to work harder. The guys could hear for themselves what needed improving, and I didn't have to be the giant pain in the butt pointing out all their mistakes.

All we needed was a name. We'd been wracking our brains for days.

I went back to my magazine, rereading the Youngbloods story.

. . . and Lowell Levinger, who calls himself "Banana" . . .

Banana. For some reason, it really struck me. I liked it.

The Bananas? Nah. Too stupid.

The Banana?

That was kind of cool. Unique. But it felt like it was missing something. Bands on the radio and in the magazines had really fancy names, weird names, like Strawberry Alarm Clock and Moby Grape and the Chocolate Watchband.

I remembered that Uncle Roy once had a band called the Swingin' Starfires. I'd always liked that name.

Swingin'. Kind of classy, like Frank Sinatra or something.

The Swingin' Banana?

I reached up and prodded the mattress above me.

Sugden's face appeared over the side. "What?"

"The Swingin' Banana. For the band. What do you think?"

Sugden almost fell out of his rack, he started laughing so hard. "Yeah, I got your swingin' banana," he said, snorting loudly between laughs. He grabbed at his glasses to keep them from falling off his face.

Driscoll lobbed a pillow at him and yelled, "You wish, Sugden!"

"Eat me!" he shouted back, still laughing.

"Yeah, like a swingin' banana!" Ioli snickered three bunks over. Sugden launched the pillow at him.

They were probably right. Everyone would take that one the wrong way.

Ioli was wiping away tears, he was laughing so hard. "Swingin' Banana—freakin' hilarious!"

"Okay, okay," I said, sliding the magazine under my bunk. "I get it. So maybe it's not the best name in the world."

"What, are you kidding?" Ioli caught his breath and tossed the pillow at me. "It's righteous!"

"You know the company would totally dig it," Jessen said, chuckling.

"What, you like it?" I asked, pulling out my calendar. I crossed out another day. Two hundred four to go.

"Heck, yeah," Sugden said. He downshifted into his best disc-jockey announcer voice. "Direct from Vietnam, please welcome . . . the Swingin' Banana!"

Applause and faux cheers erupted from all corners of the barracks. Halloran held a lighter aloft.

We were now the Swingin' Banana.

THESE BOOTS ARE
MADE FOR WALKIN'

*B*RAT-DAT-DAT-DAT-DAT!

I leaped out of my rack. There was no mistaking that sound: automatic-weapons fire. At least twenty rounds, close. Real close.

A sniper? At Dodge City?

I fumbled for my pants in the dark, memories strobing of my first night of guard duty. Everyone else was up too, half dressed, jumping for the rifle rack, grabbing the M14s. We sprinted outside. It was barely daylight, pink just starting to creep across the sky.

It had sounded like the fire came from the direction of the front gate. Smoke still hung in the air. We scanned the area outside the barracks but didn't see anything. We headed to the guard shack, now a steel shipping container with window cutouts, fortified with sandbags. Thick wisps of bluish smoke wafted from the cutouts. The sulfur smell of spent gunpowder clogged our nostrils.

I approached first. The M60 stood empty and still. There was no one behind it.

No freaking way. Charlie got the guard?

I flattened myself against the outside of the container, holding my breath. My heart hammered at my temples. *Charlie could still be in there, waiting for the next GI to grease.* I eased off the safety.

Then I heard something. It sounded like . . . whimpering?

"Oh, Mama . . . oh, Mama . . . oh, Mama . . ." Small, trembling, terrified.

It was coming from the shack.

I peered inside.

PFC Ronald Yoakum. All six feet, two hundred pounds of him, eyes big as dinner plates, was standing atop the tiny wood stool. His M14, still smoking, was aimed at the floor.

I looked down. A snake—thick, leathery, black, and probably about ten feet long before it made the mistake of crawling in to investigate the guard shack—lay in splattered segments on the ground.

I looked up at Yoakum and gently touched his arm.

"Hey, man," I said softly, "I think you got him."

Leadbetter had been sending Sergeant Hall out to find us. Sometimes we were in the barracks. Sometimes we were lined up in formation, checking in for patrol. Most times we were jamming at supply. "Captain wants to know if you're

123

ready to perform yet," Hall would say. And every time the guys all looked at me like sad, little puppy dogs.

I wanted our first show to be great. I wanted us to blow minds. I wanted it to be perfect. We were getting better, but we still weren't ready. We weren't anywhere near mind-blowing. And we had to be great.

So I always shook my head and told Sergeant Hall, "Not yet. Soon."

And Hall always rolled his eyes and marched off.

Hangar One was packed with thousands of GIs, the largest crowd I'd ever seen there. Soldiers from miles around—transportation companies, supply companies, infantry, medical—were spilling out onto the tarmac. The heavy breeze stank of diesel fuel and human waste. Artillery rumbled beyond the mountains, distant enough that no one cared.

And Nancy Sinatra still hadn't arrived.

We were guarding the dressing rooms in back. Anytime the USO brought in a show, they'd set up a stage in Hangar One—the huge covered structure at the airbase, open on all sides—and we MPs would always guard it. Some of us would patrol the airfield fence line, while others would keep an eye on the audience, and others would guard backstage. They'd bring in big stars like Ann-Margret or Martha Raye, a regular on *The Red Skelton Show*, one of my favorites.

I knew all about the USO gigs. When Dad was stationed

in Pearl Harbor with the navy in the early fifties, he was the special services officer. He brought in all kinds of Hollywood celebrities to entertain the sailors—Frank Sinatra, Dean Martin, Frankie Lane. When I was four, Mary and I hung out backstage with Bob Hope before his show. Then he went on and everybody laughed and clapped. Watching him, watching the reaction of the crowd, I was intrigued, even at four years old. He was the center of it all.

I could never figure out why the big stars came to Vietnam, though. I mean, it was hot, it was miserable, it was dangerous—why bother? Maybe they really were here for the troops. That's what we all liked to think anyway. More likely it was a tax write-off; they performed for free but charged it back on their taxes. Or maybe they just did it for the publicity.

Nancy Sinatra. I made sure I was working this show. She was a big deal because of who she was—Frank Sinatra's daughter, with the hit song "These Boots Are Made for Walkin'"—and for what she looked like—mounds of blond hair, sexy go-go booted legs, and a chest out to there. She had a kind of girl-next-door-goes-trampy thing happening, and her pin-ups were posted all over the barracks. We soldiers definitely dug her.

The waiting throng looked like a simmering kettle of green, a restless mix of anticipation and impatience. Every few minutes a roar would go up, and the soldiers would chant, "Nancy! Nancy! Nancy!"

Giant—real name Bill Martin, big guy from Illinois, over six foot—shaded his eyes with his hand, surveying the crowd. "If she doesn't show up soon, this could turn pretty ugly."

"I was thinking the same thing," I said.

We all saw a helicopter in the distance. The crowd cheered as the chopper descended to the tarmac. High-ranking officers and MPs surrounded it as Sinatra climbed out with her entourage. Giant and I craned our necks, but we couldn't see her because of all the people.

"Geez, you'd think the president had just landed," I muttered.

Giant, who had a better view because of his height, said, "I've never seen so many people traveling with a star before. Or as much military brass escorting one."

I laughed. "Guess ol' Blue Eyes said, 'Nothing better happen to my baby girl.'"

Giant chuckled. After a couple of minutes, he tapped my arm and said, "Here she comes, man, here she comes!"

When she finally made her way back to the dressing room, we barely recognized her. Her makeup was caked on two inches thick, and it was definitely starting to slide south in the heat and humidity.

"Is that her," I whispered, "or did they send somebody from the wax museum?"

Giant snickered. "She looks like a melted candle."

It didn't matter, though, because when she hit the stage

minutes later, five thousand GIs erupted with roars and whistles. She was the best thing we'd seen in a long, long while. A reminder of home, a female who was there just for us. Or so we wanted to fantasize, for an hour or so.

She was joined onstage by Jimmy Boyd, a singer and actor who did country and western tunes. The Gordian Knot, some country-rock band from Los Angeles, backed them both. They were pretty good. If we weren't all in our baggy greens with artillery thundering off in the distance, you'd think we were at an outdoor concert at the Hollywood Bowl or something. For a moment.

Boyd and Sinatra bantered back and forth, playing off of each other during the songs. Boyd must've known her pretty well, because during their act he made suggestive comments, getting huge laughs—and everything else—from the troops. She always made some smart comment back. Then she'd walk over with that big, swishy hair and those legs and give him a fake smack and the troops would go bonkers.

Nancy Sinatra had an okay voice and she sounded all right, but it was her shtick—not her singing—that was getting the soldiers all revved up. Watching thousands of GIs hooting and howling at the singer, watching her vamp it up with Jimmy Boyd, it dawned on me that maybe it wasn't really about how well you knew your material or how perfectly you played your instrument. Maybe it was about something else.

You could practice and practice until you knew your songs backward, forward, and sideways, but in the end, it was all about the show. Even when—*especially* when— you're six thousand miles away from home playing moving goddamn target for an enemy you can't freaking see, fighting a war for people you don't know and don't care to know, and who don't much care for you either.

When I got back to Dodge City, I hunted down Sergeant Hall in the orderly room.

"You can tell Captain we're ready."

THE FIRST GIG

We were all psyched.

The 127th had gone ape for the live music—lame and off-the-cuff as it was—at the farewell party at Bragg. We couldn't wait for them to see us now. We knew what we were doing. We meshed. We rocked. We even had a look, thanks to Sugden's wife. He'd written home about the band and she went out and found matching shirts for us—button-downs with flowered stripes, two in blue, two in autumn gold—and sent them over. We almost looked like a show band.

And tonight, we were going to blow the company away.

We'd spent the last hour setting things up inside the Longbranch. The amps were in place and powered up, the guitars and the Farfisa were plugged in, the mikes worked. I tested mine—"check, test, one, two, three"—one more time. Jessen was pacing behind the organ. Ioli and Sugden were laughing with Leach and McClory at the bar.

I walked over to them. "Where the heck is everybody?"

"Don't know, man." Ioli shrugged. He took a swig from his beer can.

I looked at my watch: 1900, the appointed hour. Leadbetter had made sure the company knew we were playing tonight; he'd had Sergeant Hall announce it at formation every morning this week.

Our first official gig—and there were only about twenty soldiers milling around the club.

I pointed to my watch. "It's time. Let's show 'em what we've got."

Ioli hopped off his bar stool. "Let's go!"

Sugden drained his beer.

They both followed me to the stage. We picked up our instruments and tuned up.

We were ready.

I locked eyes with each band member. Then I grinned and shouted, "Let's rock!"

"Here's one from Roy Orbison," I said into the microphone. Ioli counted it off.

And we launched into "Mean Woman Blues," "*Mmmmm, well, I got a woman, mean as she can be . . .*"

But something was wrong. I couldn't hear myself. Or the bass. Or the drums. All I could hear was organ, loud and overpowering.

The Farfisa had a collapsible booster arm underneath

the keyboard, a chrome rod with a paddle on it. You'd set your volume from the control on the keyboard, but if you took an organ solo you'd move that bar to the right with your knee to make yourself louder.

I looked over at Jessen. He had his knee against the paddle, pegged all the way to the right. I looked at his face. He was freaked. His eyes were wide, his jaw was clenched, sweat was gleaming on his forehead and ringing his collar. His hands were shaking, and he was racing through the song, throwing the other guys all off tempo.

Stage fright? I hadn't even considered it. I thought he was a concert pianist. Granted, the Longbranch was a far cry from Carnegie Hall.

We finished the mangled song and I hissed over to Jessen, "Whoa, Flash Gordon, slow down! And turn it down!"

A few of the guys in the audience clapped, Leach and McClory and Giant. Most talked and laughed among themselves. Drank their beers. Shot the breeze. We were wallpaper. This wasn't going as I'd planned.

"Sloopy" and the Monkees' "I'm a Believer" were next, Mike and Jon and I struggling to keep up as Ben sprinted through the songs. We'd never had any problems like this in practice. I couldn't figure out what was happening. But most of the audience didn't seem to care. I didn't know if that was a good thing or a bad thing.

Finally, Jessen eased up with "Mrs. Brown" by Herman's

Hermits. By the time Leadbetter made his entrance, we were sounding pretty good. Really good. "House of the Rising Sun" by the Animals. "I Fought the Law," Bobby Fuller Four, just for Captain. "Twist and Shout," Beatles. "Time Won't Let Me," Outsiders. We were tight, Jessen was cool, and it was sounding pretty hot. More and more of the troops were showing up, including Voina and Lupica and their buddies.

Great.

Captain was nodding with our beats, grinning the whole time. During a break after our first set, he made a point of speaking to us.

"You're doing a fine job, men," he said, giving Jessen a clap on the back.

"Thank you, sir," Ben said.

"Thanks for letting us put it together," I added.

"It's just what we needed around here." Captain lit up his pipe. "Looks like the soldiers are really enjoying it."

"We hope so, sir," I said, though I still wasn't convinced.

"Carry on, then." Leadbetter moved off to circulate through the Longbranch, shaking guys' hands and slapping backs.

"Hey, man, sounds great. Can I buy you a beer?"

Voina. We hadn't crossed paths too much since we'd arrived in Dodge City. He and his buddies were in Second Platoon; they ran on a different schedule than we did. He put out his hand and I shook it.

132

"Thanks," I said. "I don't drink, but I'll take a Coke." I wasn't sure how Voina would be about the band. Was he pissed because we hadn't asked him to join? Did he think he should be a part of it since he played guitar too?

"Not my style, but you guys are rockin'," he said, smiling. He handed me the soda. I could tell he was sincere. There wasn't a hint of jealousy or anger on his face. He was obviously fine with it.

Cool. Lupica can kiss my butt.

Voina and I talked a bit about the instruments and the equipment. He especially liked the bamboo mike stands. "Pretty resourceful," he said.

"Thanks, man. You know, when in Vietnam . . ." I said, glancing at my watch. "Looks like it's time for the second set."

"Good deal," Voina said. "Hey, break a leg, man."

The band powered through a second and third set, the guys in the audience getting more responsive as they got more sloshed. Voina clapped and hollered, even shouted out a request for Elvis. Good thing Presley did "Mean Woman Blues" too; we played it again just for Voina. Lupica and his boys tried to look bored, never clapping, acting as if we weren't even there.

Screw 'em.

Still, the response to the Banana's first big gig wasn't what I'd hoped for. Adequate, I guess, but hardly overwhelming. What the hell happened? Where was half the company? They loved us when we weren't even a band. Maybe the guys were tired of us already. Everybody'd heard us practicing out in the supply tent for the last four weeks, whether they'd wanted to or not. Or maybe we weren't doing the songs they wanted to hear. But, damn, we were playing everything they listened to on the radio, plus some old classics. My head started to hurt.

"Woo-wee, baby, we smoked 'em!" Ioli shouted as we wrapped up our third hour. He stood to stretch, and he and Sugden exchanged high fives.

"Rocked and rolled, buddy, rocked and rolled," Jessen said, coming out from behind the organ, grabbing Ioli by the neck and giving him a playful noogie.

Sugden put down his bass and sparked up a cigarette. "So, what'd you think, Dean?" he said, exhaling.

I shrugged. I didn't want to spoil anybody's post-concert high. "Yeah, it was good."

Ioli trotted over. "What, you don't think it was good? It was freakin' good! You don't think it was good? I'm telling you, it was good!"

"Yeah, I know, I know, it was good, okay?" I said, returning my guitar to its case. I slammed the case shut. *Geez, enough.* "Didn't I just say it was good?"

Jessen grabbed a beer from behind the Farfisa. "Well, you're acting like you think it sucked."

I took a deep breath and held it. Let it out. I unplugged my amp.

"It's just not the reaction I expected," I finally said, winding the cord.

"What? They dug it!" Ioli said. "Didn't you hear them clapping and yelling?"

I didn't say anything as I started breaking down my microphone.

"Oh, I get it," Jessen said. "You wanted them dancing on the tables, like back at Bragg."

"Swinging from the rafters," Sugden added. "Right?"

I didn't know what I wanted. Just something . . . more. What was wrong with these guys? Where was everybody? Didn't these ungrateful assholes get what had been done for them? We chased down all the equipment, invested our own money, practiced all these weeks. For what? To be the background noise at the enlisted men's club?

I didn't care if we ever played for the company again.

I grabbed my gear and turned for the door.

"Yeah. Something like that."

MACV

oli was walking back from the motor pool, hot and sweaty after checking in his patrol jeep. He was excited.

"I just talked to a guy who said there's a lieutenant over at MACV who handles the entertainment for all the army clubs in the area," he said as he pulled off his helmet. "He said that this guy could probably book us into some clubs."

"Play other clubs?" I said. "For other companies?"

That was something I'd never even thought about. We weren't even sure the Banana was authorized to perform for Dodge City's troops, let alone any others. Yeah, Leadbetter was making it work. But I was pretty certain the Army Code of Conduct never said anything about rock bands.

And judging from the company's reaction to our first gig, I wasn't sure I ever wanted to play for military guys again.

Still, I couldn't help but wonder if maybe it would be

different somewhere else . . . with a different audience . . .

I shook my head. "I don't know, man." We headed to the mess hall.

But I just couldn't let the idea go.

MACV. Military Assistance Command, Vietnam. Command structure for all U.S. military in-country. The big guns.

I pulled the patrol jeep up to the gate.

"Need to speak with the lieutenant in charge of Morale, Welfare, and Recreation," I told the guard, trying my best to sound official.

"That's Steinmetz, to the rear." To my surprise, he gave me directions and waved me through.

I parked in front of the whitewashed stucco office building at the back of the compound and walked in.

The lieutenant was at his desk. When he saw my MP uniform, he jumped up, obviously thinking there was trouble.

"No problems, sir," I said as I saluted. Steinmetz looked relieved. He returned my salute and sat back down.

"Well, then, what can I do for you, Specialist"—he squinted at the name on my pocket—"Kohler?" He offered me a cigarette from a metal box on his desk.

I politely waved it away. I could hardly believe I was going through with this.

"Sir, I understand you book all the entertainment for

the army clubs in the area," I said.

"That's right." He blew a smoke ring. It rose, then vanished.

What the hell am I doing?

"Well, I have a band," I said.

The cigarette froze in midair. The lieutenant looked stunned.

Okay, we're sunk. Way to go, Kohler.

"A band?" His eyes narrowed as if he didn't believe me. "What kind of band?"

"A rock band, sir."

Stay calm, stay calm. What's the worst he can do to us— send us to Vietnam?

"Is that so?" he said slowly, still digesting my information. His chair creaked and he leaned forward over his desk to give me a closer look. "And what does your band play, Specialist Kohler?"

Okay, I'm in deep. No backing out now.

"Stuff that's on the radio, sir," I said. "Beatles, Rolling Stones, the Animals."

His jaw dropped.

Damn. Now I've gone and done it. It's the end of the Banana. Maybe he'll transfer us up to the front line, keep us too busy staying alive to think about making music. Damn it, Kohler, couldn't you leave well enough alone?

The lieutenant frowned and tamped out his cigarette in a heavy glass ashtray on the corner of his desk. He stood up.

Here it comes.

Without a word, he walked over to a massive scheduling chart on the wall behind his desk. He picked up a marker, handed it to me, and said, "I've got sixteen clubs. You pick out where you want to be and when you want to be there."

It took me a couple of seconds to register what he'd just said.

"There's only one catch," he continued, leaning back against the desk. "Your first gig will be right here. There's an officers' club upstairs for the brass on the compound." He folded his arms. "I want to check you out."

An audition. I nodded, still not believing what I was hearing.

"Now, assuming I like your band, when can you men play?"

I found my voice.

"Well, sir," I began, "we've all got three-day patrols that happen in a row. Then we have three midnight to oh-eight hundred patrols. So on those nights, we could probably perform up until about twenty-two hundred. Maybe nineteen hundred to twenty-two hundred?" I quickly scrawled some dates onto the chart, my mind racing.

The lieutenant was nodding.

"And how much do you want, Specialist?" he asked.

How much do I want? Like money? I could've been wrong, but it sounded like he actually wanted to pay us for our gigs. I thought fast—back home with the Satellites we made sixty dollars a night, more every once in a while.

"A hundred bucks a show," I blurted.

Steinmetz extended a hand. "No problem, Specialist Kohler," he said as we shook. "You got it."

"You gotta be kidding me, Kohler," Captain Leadbetter said. He hooked his thumbs inside his web belt, his feet planted wide in the red dirt outside the Longbranch, where he was supervising construction of an outdoor patio, complete with white picket fence and striped umbrellas.

Dodge City was starting to look like a country club. I thought of the guys out in the bush, of Joynes, of Goodridge, and felt guilty. Vietnam was no freakin' country club for them.

"No, sir." I cleared my throat. "The lieutenant said we could play all of his clubs. We just have to audition at MACV first."

The captain was silent. I couldn't tell what he was thinking. The work detail hammered behind him.

I clasped my hands behind my back, trying to keep from fidgeting.

"So what do you say, sir?" I nudged. I tried the pity-the-broke-soldiers angle, figuring it couldn't hurt. "The equipment was really expensive. We paid for it ourselves. Some outside jobs would really help defray our costs, sir."

We needed his permission . . . and a way to get all of our equipment there.

"Can we do it, sir?"

The captain reached up under his cover and scratched his head. He closed his eyes and pinched the bridge of his nose. Then he exhaled, slowly, loudly.

"All right, soldier," he finally said. "You can do the gig. It smacks of unauthorized use, but I'm gonna let you take one of the three-quarter-ton pickup trucks. Now, before you go and get too excited, let me tell you the way it's gonna be. You're gonna go straight from here to the gig and back. No stops, no detours. You will have no weapons. And you're gonna wear your fatigues all the way there and all the way back. You change into your civilian clothes at the gig. You got that, Specialist?"

Holy crap, we're going to play for MACV.

"Yes, sir, Captain, sir," I said, trying to hide my smile.

"Good. Now don't let me down. Dismissed."

I saluted and turned to leave.

"Oh, and Kohler," Captain said.

"Yes, sir?"

He raised a fist and threw a mock uppercut in the air.

"Knock 'em dead."

19

THE ELECTRICAL BANANA

"Look, this gig is major." I picked up my guitar and started to tune it. "Our foot in the door to all sorts of other gigs, paying gigs. What happens when that MACV lieutenant hears that our band's called the Swingin' Banana?"

"He'll get hungry for some fruit?" Ioli said. "Or maybe a pie?" He was on his knees, tightening up his bass drumhead.

Jessen leaned over the organ's case, his chin in his hands. "He'll start swinging from the trees?"

"He'll think we're a joke, that's what," I said. "The name has to change. Now, come on, you guys. Think."

It was quiet, except for the faint hum of the amplifiers and the buzz of mosquitoes lurking in the supply tent's shadows.

Ben broke the silence. "How about the Banana Boys?"

We groaned. "You're kidding, right?" Sugden lounged on the supply cot, bass across his chest.

"The Banana Split?" Ioli offered. "With whipped cream and nuts and a big, fat cherry on top. Man, I'm starving."

Sugden sat up. "What about the Electric Banana?"

We let it sink in for a second.

"Hey, that's kinda cool," Jessen said.

Ioli nodded. "Yeah, not bad."

"I dig it," I said. I plugged my guitar into my amp. "Okay, it's settled. We're the Electric Banana. Now, let's get to work."

Leach walked in, his reel-to-reel tucked under his arm.

"Hey, Jim," Jessen called out, "today you're taping the very first practice of the Electric Banana."

"Electric Banana?" Leach placed the tape recorder on an empty ammo crate. "You mean, like the Electric Prunes? 'I Had Too Much to Dream'?"

Sugden fell back on the cot. "Damn."

"I forgot about those guys," Ioli said.

"Back to the drawing board," I said.

The next day I was cleaning my rifle back at the barracks. Suttle had his record player going upstairs. Donovan's "Mellow Yellow" wafted through the screen door. *Electrical banana/ Is gonna be a sudden craze . . ."*

I put down my brush. *That's it.*

The Electrical Banana.

At practice that afternoon, the guys approved the name. Then I told them I was thinking about band uniforms,

143

something a little more elaborate than the button-down shirts, something that had some visual flair. Like what a show band would wear.

Ioli piped up. "I've seen some tailor shops downtown. They could measure us, custom-make us something. Probably wouldn't be that much dough."

So the four of us headed downtown and found a tailor. I'd brought along a magazine picture of Herman's Hermits, the British band with the big hits "I'm into Something Good" and "Mrs. Brown, You've Got a Lovely Daughter." In the photo, the Hermits' front man, Peter Noone, had on a shirt with blousy sleeves, kind of a buccaneer-looking thing. We all thought it looked cool.

"What I do for GI Number One?" Papasan at the tailor shop asked us.

I showed him the picture. "We want outfits that look like this," I told him. "Shirts. And pants too. All the same color. Yellow."

We weren't sure he understood. We looked around the shop and found a bolt of yellow fabric. "Like this," we said.

Papasan nodded and measured us. Then he held up three fingers.

"GI come back," he said.

So after three days, we went back. Four beautifully tailored band uniforms were waiting for us. None of us had ever worn clothes that fit so well.

All for twelve bucks.

* * *

We followed all the rules.

No stops, no detours.

No weapons.

Fatigues on the way, then change into our band uniforms.

We were on the second floor of the MACV building in a cavernous room, like a mess hall, with a stage on one end. There were assorted tables and chairs, a bar along one side, a banquet table with seating for thirty at the far end of the room. A few junior officers were milling around when we arrived. As we set up our equipment, they looked at us like we were from Mars. They clearly had no idea who we were or what we were doing there.

I felt a nervous twinge in my stomach.

"Are we in the right place, man?" Sugden asked in a low voice as he pulled his bass from its case and started to tune up.

I locked my microphone onto its bamboo stand. "I think so."

I hope so. I looked around for Lieutenant Steinmetz.

Soon, other officers arrived, the higher ranks. They were escorting Vietnamese women, all dressed up like they were going to a fancy nightclub—high heels, sequins, lots of eyeliner, and red lipstick. They headed to the banquet table. Chairs scraped as the officers pulled them out for the women.

"Looks like they're expecting a really big show," Ioli said from behind the drums, his voice sounding unsure.

"Yeah, don't they know we're just a rock band?" Jessen asked. He was pacing behind the organ, his hair damp with sweat already. Rings of perspiration were forming under his arms.

I was starting to worry that the Electrical Banana might not be up for this after all. Maybe it was too soon. Maybe we needed more practice. Maybe this was going to be another fiasco.

Where the hell is Steinmetz?

"Come on, guys, they want a big show," I said, trying to sound positive. "Then let's give 'em one. We rock, remember?"

The guys exchanged uneasy glances. This wasn't looking too good.

I scanned the rapidly filling hall. Still no sign of Steinmetz.

"I need a beer," Sugden said, leaning his bass against the wall. He jumped offstage.

"Me too," Ioli said.

"Me three," parroted Jessen. He and Mike followed Jon like ducklings over to the bartender.

Great. Our first big concert date, and my band's at the bar.

The twinge turned to full-fledged butterflies as I checked and rechecked all the cord connections to the amps. The fluttering in my stomach reminded me of the first real gig of my life, with the Mustangs, at the opening of the neighborhood Little League baseball season. They'd set us up on two sheets of plywood out on the field, let us play three songs. I never forgot how it felt that first time. Climbing onto that makeshift stage to show the audience what you're made of. Scared as hell, hoping your shaking fingers will cooperate. Part nerves, part excitement—pure adrenaline. Like now.

I gave the equipment one last check and headed over to the bar, where Sugden, Ioli, and Jessen were draining their beers. I ordered a Coke, and went over the set list a few times in my head.

"So this is it," Ioli said, raising his voice over the chattering crowd. "The big audition. You guys ready to kill it?"

Sugden put out his cigarette. "Damn straight." He raised his beer can. "To the Banana—long may it wave!"

Ioli lifted his can. "Let's do it, baby!"

Jessen raised his. "Ba-na-na!" he hooted.

"Showtime!" I added, clinking their cans with mine.

I didn't know if it was the beer talking or what, but the guys sounded revved. The butterflies settled. We hopped up onstage.

"Here's one from Roy Orbison," I said, and we launched into "Mean Woman Blues." The first chords echoed through the hall and I knew immediately that we'd nailed it. Ben was fine, leaning into the keys, sliding the volume paddle on his solos. Ioli was swinging like Ringo Starr,

147

and Sugden was coolly thumping out the undertone. We had all the younger officers' attention—heads were nodding in tempo, feet were tapping on the floor, fingers were drumming on the tables.

More and more brass streamed in. Out of the corner of my eye, I saw Steinmetz. He strolled to the end of the bar. He was watching us, watching the crowd, gauging their reaction. The applause grew louder and heartier with every song.

This is good. We're doing it.

I looked around at the band. I could tell they knew it. Sure, no one was dancing on the tables, but these were officers. Conduct unbecoming or whatever. But we were on; we sounded hot. And everybody was digging it.

After the second set, Lieutenant Steinmetz found me leaning against the stage, discussing what to put in the third set with Sugden.

"Sir?" I said.

"Nice job, men," he said, shaking our hands. "The officers are really enjoying themselves."

Yes.

"Thank you, sir," I said.

"Do you still want to play my clubs?"

I stole a look at Sugden. He raised his eyebrows and nodded.

"Yes, sir. We really do, sir."

"Fine, then," Steimetz said. "The shows are yours."

Toward the end of the third set, one of the sequined Vietnamese girls walked up to the stage with a piece of paper. I thought it was a song request.

"Lynda at Lyndabar wants to see you," she said between songs, handing me the note.

Lynda? At Lyndabar? What does that mean? All I could think to say was, "Right now?"

"Come see her," the girl said with a little smile, and walked away.

I looked down at the piece of paper. On it was written LYNDABAR and an address.

"What's that?" Ioli called from behind the drums.

I walked over to him, puzzled. "She said Lynda at Lyndabar wants me to come see her." I didn't drink, I wasn't a bar guy. Ioli and Jessen and Sugden, they knew all the downtown watering holes. "What's the Lyndabar?"

Ioli snorted, "Lynda? At the Lyndabar? Wants to see you?" It was as if Elizabeth Taylor herself had summoned me to her lair—totally preposterous.

The other guys burst out laughing.

"What?" I said. My cheeks started to burn.

20

LYNDA

I kept the note in my pocket, along with my calendar.

The guys razzed me all week. "Do I hear Lynda calling?" or "Wonder what Lynda wants?" they'd crack, making wolf whistles and cutting up. Whenever I'd ask anyone about the Lyndabar, they'd get a dumb Cheshire Cat grin and say, "You'll find out." I had a feeling I knew what it was all about. But I wasn't sure. When I finally got fed up with all the stupid wisecracks, I decided to go down there one afternoon to see for myself.

I found it, a low-slung building bookended by tacky trinket shops. The sign said LYNDABAR in large red letters across the front, with LYNDA THE STEAKHOUSE in smaller letters underneath.

So it's a restaurant. What's the big deal?

I walked in the front door. I blinked as my eyes adjusted to the darkness. The place smelled of stale beer, cigarettes, and cooking grease. Men, some Vietnamese, most American, were seated at tables or at the bar, smoking, drinking, laughing loudly. They eyed me briefly. I was in my civvies, so I was no threat. Vietnamese girls in high heels and short skirts served the men beer. Some sat with them, others left with them through a back door strung with hanging beads. The surf-guitar twang of the Ventures pumped meekly from a portable stereo behind the bar, its faded plastic speakers hung high on the stucco wall.

A waitress in heavy eye makeup walked up to me. Like all Vietnamese women, she couldn't have been much taller than four feet.

"I get you drink, handsome?" she said. "You buy me Saigon tea?"

Oh. Okay. Got it. So maybe the guys were right.

I was still curious, though. And I knew I'd never live it down back at the barracks if I didn't at least meet this Lynda. She was probably some old, fat madame with warts and facial hair.

"I'm here to see Lynda," I told the waitress. "She asked me to come. I'm in a band."

I saw a spark of recognition in her eyes—she must've been at the MACV gig too. She scampered to the back.

I took a seat at the bar and ordered a Coke.

Soon Lynda came out. She wasn't old or fat. She was gorgeous. Blue-black hair down her back, a heavy fringe of bangs over inky almond eyes.

Lynda sat on the stool next to me and crossed her legs, the slit of her skirt revealing slender calf to thigh. I noticed her fishnet hose had a hole at one knee and the heels of her snakeskin stilettos were worn. She held a long cigarette between her slim fingers, the nails ragged red at the tips. I couldn't take my eyes from her. She looked mysterious. Dangerous. I wanted to touch her.

Trust no one. Isn't that what Wash had said?

"I am glad that you came," she said, and I felt like I was falling downhill, not able to stop. "I enjoyed your band very much at MACV. I was sad that I had to leave early to get back to the business here. That's why I sent one of the girls with the note. I hope that wasn't too forward?"

My tongue felt stuck to the roof of my mouth. I couldn't believe it. She'd liked our gig, she was beautiful, she spoke excellent English, not the fractured pidgin of most locals. This wasn't what I'd expected at all.

Say something, Kohler.

"Forward? Oh, no, it was fine."

"How old are you—um—?" She laughed. Not a coy bar-girl giggle. A woman's laugh. It sounded like a song. "I'm sorry, I don't even know your name."

"I'm Dean."

"Dean," she repeated slowly.

"I'm twenty," I said.

She tilted her head and gave me a teasing smile. "Oh, an older man."

I laughed. It sounded nervous. "Why? How old are you?"

"Nineteen," she said, soft and low.

I wasn't sure I believed it. She didn't act like she was nineteen. And how could someone that young have her own bar? Ioli and Sugden had said they thought she owned a seamstress shop too. I studied her face for a moment. She kind of looked nineteen, but there was something about her eyes, a hardness, that made her seem years older.

She took a drag of her cigarette. "So how long will you and your band be in town? Will you be heading back to the States soon, or are you on tour?"

I laughed again. I couldn't help it. She thought we were a real band, a rock band on a concert tour of the world. I didn't know if I should tell her the truth or live out the fantasy with her.

"We're here for a while," I said, still chuckling.

She gave me a confused smile. "You are? Well, that is wonderful, Dean. I love American rock and roll. You hear the Ventures playing, yes? You like the Ventures?"

She brightened as we talked about music. She knew all the current songs and bands. She was intelligent and funny and we ended up sitting there talking for two hours.

When I finally told her I needed to get going, she excused herself and disappeared into the back. She returned holding a thick Sears catalog, its pages dog-eared and worn. She set it down on the counter, opened it to the middle, and pulled out an order form. It was neatly filled out in ballpoint ink with several rows' worth of item codes. She handed it to me.

"You are a good friend," she said, touching my forearm. The hairs rose and prickled. "You will get these things for me?"

Huh? This is weird. We've known each other for a couple of hours and she's already asking me to buy her stuff?

I looked at the form. She'd listed some clothes, fishnet stockings, shoes. The grand total: thirty-eight dollars.

She probably can't get stuff like that around here. After all, it's a war zone. And Vietnamese probably can't send mail to the U.S. or she would have ordered it herself. Or maybe this is her way of getting closer to me. Or maybe it's a come-on. Or maybe—the goose bumps lingered—*if I did her a favor . . .*

I took the form with me back to Dodge City. I'd send it off to Mom, I decided. I wasn't sure what Mom was going to think. And I didn't really want to explain. What if she saw Judy and let something slip?

"Sears catalog!" Ioli snorted back at the barracks, snatching the form from my hand. I grabbed for it, but he was in the mood for a game of keep-away. I sat on my bunk.

"You go down to the Lyndabar—the *Lyndabar*—and you're talking Sears catalog?" Ioli guffawed, handing the paper off to Sugden, who was polishing both his rifle and his bass on his bunk.

Suttle's record player was on upstairs. ". . . *And the beat goes on . . .*" Sonny and Cher.

I sighed and lay back on my pillow, arms behind my head. It was best to ride this one out.

"Oh, Deanie-boy," Sugden trilled in his best girlie voice, crossing his legs and fanning himself with the form, "would you be a good little monkey and do my shopping for me? Let's see, I need stockings . . ."

Ioli grabbed the form back from Sugden. He fanned his pants.

". . . and panties and brassieres . . ."

Jessen snatched the paper from Ioli.

". . . and how about a leash?" he said in a singsong voice, twirling down the middle of the barracks waving the form above his head. "A nice, pink leash, just for Deanie-boy, my favorite little oochie-koochie monkey."

Sugden screeched like an ape.

Jessen wagged his finger at the guys. "Do as I say and you just might get some!" he warbled. He stopped at my bunk and dropped the form. It fluttered to my chest.

"Very funny, asswipes," I muttered, sitting up and stuffing the order slip into an envelope. "Jessen, I give your little dance number there a nine."

"Why, thank you, Deanie," he cooed, batting his eyelashes. He attempted a curtsy, but Ioli tackled him. They wrestled on the floor.

Leach had let me borrow his reel-to-reel again. I grabbed

155

for the headphones, put them over my ears, and switched on a Banana tape I was planning to send to Roy. It was the closest thing to privacy in a barracks full of comedians. I scribbled off a quick note asking Mom to please mail the order form, and that I'd pay her back when I got home.

Mom came through.

In a couple of weeks the package from Sears arrived.

I brought it on patrol the next day and dropped by the Lyndabar to deliver it.

Lynda was behind the bar. "Dean, you are here!" she said when she saw me, putting a hand to her mouth. "I did not know if I would see you again."

I'd thought about her every day since we'd met. She was unlike any other female I'd ever known. And I wasn't sure if that was good or bad. I knew what her business was, or I thought I knew. I knew what her waitresses did. But Lynda wasn't like that, I was sure. Lynda was no sleazy bar girl. She was different. She had class. She was smart. Exciting.

"And you're . . . a GI?" She sounded stunned.

I'd forgotten that she'd never seen me in uniform. I'd been in the Banana outfit at MACV, and street clothes here at the Lyndabar.

"Afraid so," I said. I couldn't read her face. She'd moved her hand to her cheek.

"But the band? The rock and roll?"

"Something we do in our spare time." I put my helmet

down on the bar counter.

She looked at it. "MP? Dean, you are Military Police?"

"Yes, ma'am." I handed her the package. "Here, this is for you."

She looked at it and her eyes got shiny. "Oh . . ." she said softly, touching the Sears logo in the corner. She looked up at me and smiled, blinking away tears. "Thank you, Dean. Thank you so much."

It was as if she figured I'd changed my mind and thrown her order form away or something. As if I'd forgotten all about her.

She slipped behind the bar and pulled some money from the cash register. She tried to slide a stack of folded bills into my shirt pocket. I wouldn't let her. I grabbed her hand, placed the money on her palm, and closed those red nails around it.

From then on, I dropped by during the day a couple times a week, stopping in on patrol. Lynda couldn't be any happier. Having an MP regularly checking on your place was good for business. The customers knew things would stay under control. The Cong would think twice about trying to turn the bar owner. And the bar owner wouldn't have to worry about her establishment landing on the army's crap list.

One afternoon as I headed back out to the jeep, Lynda grabbed my arm. She moved in close, lifting her lips toward my ear. I smelled her warmth—musky, electric.

"You come see me tomorrow night. Yes?"

TROUBLE

If I got caught, I'd be in deep trouble. Real deep.

"Pops" Whitney—at twenty-eight, the company elder—would be too, for dropping me off on his way to patrol. The rules were that downtown was off-limits after 1900 hours to all military except ambulances, emergency vehicles, and MPs. Here it was almost 2000 hours, and I was in my street clothes out in front of the Lyndabar. Totally UA, unauthorized absence. Pops would be back before dawn to pick me up and get us to Dodge City before roll call. Nobody would be the wiser. If I didn't get caught.

The street was dark. Locals stared at me from doorways and shuttered storefronts, their eyes cold, suspicious. They turned to one another and jabbered and laughed in their high, creepy voices, then darted away.

Charlie? Sympathizers? My eyes did a jittery dance, up the sidewalk and back, the black alleys. I wished for my

MP uniform and gun.

I ducked inside. The bar was after-hours dim. Empty.

Lynda was waiting for me. She kissed me. Deep. Hard. We danced, slow, Jim Morrison in the background begging his baby to light his fire.

She took my hand and led me through the back, past a small, greasy kitchen, an office and liquor storeroom, and out another door that opened onto a courtyard. A cinder-block wall about ten feet high enclosed the area. Three old Vietnamese—men? women? I couldn't tell in the dark—sat around a blazing bonfire in the center of the yard, hunched in their chairs. Purple shadows skulked across the cinder blocks. Rusting nails, sharp points up, and shards of broken glass capping the wall glinted in the firelight, scratching at the black sky.

Lynda led me through the courtyard. The geezers by the fire didn't even look up. We walked past a row of what looked like four small motel rooms. Seedy, low-rent motel rooms. I heard vague thumping noises, muffled moans.

Oh. Yeah. Okay. So that's where they go. But Lynda doesn't do that. She's different. Isn't she?

We stopped at a small, private hut at the farthest corner of the courtyard. Behind it I could see a crude outdoor shower, a rain barrel up on stilts over an L-shaped enclosure.

Lynda opened the door and pulled me in.

* * *

159

I was in deep trouble. Real deep.

Two hours to roll call and no sign of Pops. To the east, the sky was starting to brighten. In the thin light, across the street, I could see three figures huddled together. They stared over at me. Cowboys—sulky Vietnamese kids who zipped around on their motor scooters, cutting off traffic, playing chicken with the military vehicles.

U.S. Army MPs in Nam Rule #532: No military personnel on the natives' motorbikes. Too many of our guys had gotten killed falling off the back.

But it was my only option.

I flagged one of the cowboys over. After a few minutes of persuading, plus a crisp five-dollar bill, he agreed to give me a ride back to base. I climbed on behind him, me all of one hundred thirty-five pounds, the kid about half that. Lyndabar was on the far side of town; it took us nearly half an hour to get over to Dodge City.

The sky was lavender when I motioned the cowboy to stop a few hundred yards from the front gate. I didn't want him getting shot; I didn't need me getting shot either. The cowboy drove off.

Great. I'm here. Now what?

The way I figured it, there were three possible scenarios. One: The guy pulling guard duty behind the M60 would mistake me for the enemy and wax my ass. Two: The guy pulling guard duty would report my UA butt, the band would be history, and I'd be sent to cool my heels with the rest of the army's screwups at Long Binh jail. Three: The guy pulling guard duty was a buddy and would cover for me.

I took a deep breath. Time to spin the big wheel of luck.

I stood in the road and yelled at the gate.

"Don't shoot! Friendly! It's Kohler!"

I heard a snicker.

"Dean, that you?"

Lupica. He burst out laughing.

Damn.

I went through the rest of the day waiting for the firestorm. Nothing. In the mess hall, when Leadbetter stopped by our table, I thought I was done for. But he just slapped me on the back and said the band's practices were sounding great. Maybe Lupica was going to keep our little secret. I hoped so, but I definitely wasn't planning on it. One more thing to worry about.

Mail call that afternoon had brought another tape from Uncle Roy. With Leach letting me borrow his reel-to-reel, Roy and I had been sending recordings back and forth. That evening after chow, I switched on the tape.

"Hey, Dean, it's Uncle Roy. How are you, buddy? Hope you're keeping your head down over there. We all watch the news every night and we're always thinking of you.

"So your Mom had herself a conniption when she saw what you were buying from Sears. Thought you were pick-

ing up some interesting new tastes in fashion, if you know what I mean. Don't worry, though, your Dad set her straight. Navy lifer, he knows what's going on, sport. Your Mom hopes you're being careful, if you know what I mean. Good to know you're not getting too lonely over there, though, ha-ha!

"So how's the band going? Thanks for the tape, sounds like you guys are really starting to gel.

"Listen, Dean, I wanted to let you know about something that's been going on. And, now, I don't want you getting steamed about this, so hear me out. See, what happened was, after you left, I got Danny Darden to take your place in the Satellites. You remember him, he used to be in the Camaros?

"Now, Dean, I know what you're thinking, so just sit down and keep listening. You know we had that offer from Tower, and you know we had to pass it up because of you getting drafted and all. But look, buddy, I didn't want to lose that opportunity for you. I thought maybe if I could keep the Satellites together, we could still keep that door open, you know what I mean?

"Let me tell you, Dean, Danny Darden, he just didn't work out. Never got the hang of your songs, just couldn't sing 'em the right way. Guess I should've known it wouldn't be the same. Granted, he gave it a good try, a real good try. Even in the studio.

"Now, Dean, settle down. Yes, I put 'em in the studio. I thought that maybe if Tower heard the new Satellites, they *might put the offer back on the table, you know? We'd sign the deal, and then when you come home, well, of course we'd get you back in and work it all out.*

"I know what you're probably thinking right now, buddy. But it ain't true. I wasn't selling you out or anything. No way. You were always going to be a part of the Satellites. Heck, it's your band, right?

"But you know what, Dean, it doesn't really matter, see. Tower didn't like the new stuff. Can't say's I blame them. Danny Darden's fine, but he's not Dean Kohler, you know? So I'm sorry, buddy, I tried. But the record thing, looks like it's just not part of the plan right now.

"But, hey, listen, the most important thing is getting you back home safe and sound, right? And, you know, we'll put something together when you get back. You can count on it. You keep writing those songs and we'll find you an album deal, that's what we'll do. Heck, Tower's just one record company. And if they liked your stuff, well, there's plenty of other places we can try. . . ."

I switched off the tape and yanked the headphones. I was boiling.

Danny Darden? What the hell? Fronting my band? Singing my songs? Recording them? The Satellites were my band. Not Roy's. What the hell was he thinking?

Roy was just trying to salvage the Tower deal any way he could. Wouldn't I have been doing exactly the same thing?

I ran a hand over my face, took a deep breath, and lay

back on my bunk. I studied the metal ceiling. I was glad everyone else was off breaking in the new outdoor movie screen Leadbetter'd authorized for us. The dull rumble of H & I fire—harassment and interdictment, the army jerking Charlie's chain—echoed beyond the mountain. It almost didn't bother me anymore; the rifles were ready in their rack. It was background noise, like some weird film sound-track.

The enemy was out there somewhere—not close but definitely out there—and I didn't care. I wondered how that could be. Was I getting used to—*war*? Anything could be familiar if you lived with it long enough. Was I a true soldier now, a feelings-free, combat-ready robot? Was that what I was turning into?

All of a sudden, I didn't know who I was. I was in a free fall through my own life. I had left the person I had been far behind.

I squeezed my eyes shut.

If there was ever any doubt, the recording contract was now officially history. That particular window of opportunity had been slammed shut. Loudly.

And Dean Kohler as I'd known him was over. There was no going back.

Deal with it.

I turned to the wall. I watched a fat, gray spider make its ascent. I pulled the pillow around my head.

My eyes didn't close for hours.

22

96 Tears

I t was the Banana's first gig for enlisted troops—the military's lowest ranks: the working force, like us—and I wasn't looking forward to it. We'd gone over just fine with the officers at MACV. But enlisted men, they'd be a tough crowd. If they showed up at all. The weak turnout at our Dodge City debut replayed in my mind. I sighed as I turned the truck into the entrance of the 64th Transportation Company.

"Here it is, you guys," Ioli said excitedly from the passenger side. "We're gonna rock 'em!" I wished I felt as optimistic.

I drove up to the gate. When I told the bored-looking guard who we were and why we were there, his face lit up. "No kidding?" He checked out the back of the truck, piled high with drums, amps, guitars, Sugden, and Jessen. "All right, man! What kind of stuff do you guys play?"

"Rock and roll," I said. I was surprised by his enthusiasm. "You should check it out if you can," I added.

"Righteous," he said. "My shift ends in an hour. I'll be there. Club's straight back, then take your second left." He waved us through.

"Well, we can count on at least one guy showing up," I muttered.

"Ease up, man," Sugden said through the open rear window. "It's gonna be cool."

We rolled up to the club.

"Looks empty," I said. "Great."

Jessen reached in and thumped me on the head. "Man, it's early. Relax."

"Wonder where they want us to load in?" I said.

Ioli hopped down. "Let me check it out." He ran inside. Soon he came back out with the club manager.

"Great to see you!" the guy said, pumping my hand like I was some sort of celebrity. "The Electrical Banana—awesome! Can't believe you guys are here. If you pull your truck around back, you can bring your stuff in through that door. Do you need a hand? I can get you some extra bodies to help carry your gear. Anybody need a drink?"

We all looked at one another. Maybe this wasn't going to be so bad after all.

We unpacked our stuff and set up onstage, stacking the cases in a back corner. Then we tuned up. Jessen hit the notes for us on the Farfisa, and Sugden and I tuned our guitars to him and each other. After our sound check—a quick run-through of the Yardbirds' "Heart Full of Soul" to make sure all the instruments, amplifiers, and connections were tuned and working—Jessen called us over.

"I've been working on this at night, with the headphones on. Listen."

He played the basic organ part to "96 Tears." We were amazed. It was a song we really wanted to add to our set list, but we were having a lot of trouble figuring out. We just couldn't get the chord changes in the middle.

"Does that sound right to you?" Ben asked when he was finished.

"Yeah, man, just like the record," Ioli said with a grin.

"How'd you figure it out, Einstein?" Sugden asked.

Ben shrugged. "It's an organ song, not a guitar song, so I guess it was just easier for me to pick it apart. One more thing," Ben added. "I learned the organ solo on 'House of the Rising Sun' too, so if you guys can give me some space in the song tonight, I can do a little showing off myself."

"You got it," I said as we filed off the stage. I gave Jessen a clap on the back. I was proud of him. "You've been doing your homework, man."

"Well, it gives me something to think about," Ben said. He looked down for a second, then looked back at me. "You know, so I don't have to think about—other stuff."

I nodded, knowing just what he meant.

* * *

1600. A packed house.

A packed house.

The club was jammed with guys in baggy greens. All the tables were filled and it was standing room only along the walls. The club had been talking up the show all week, the manager told us. It looked like their promotion definitely worked.

The crowd cheered as we ripped into the Rivieras' rowdy "California Sun." By the end of the song we knew we had them by the guitar strings. All of us in the band were on, soaking up the applause, feeding off of it, and the rolling energy from each song flowed right into the next. "Mrs. Brown," by the Hermits; "Money," the Kingsmen; "Roll Over Beethoven," Chuck Berry; "Hitchhike," the Stones— the first set felt like a locomotive rocketing out of the station, the shouting crowd hanging on for the rip-roaring ride. It was intense, we all fed off the rush—players and audience— and for the first time in a long while I remembered what performing was really all about.

At the break, Ioli, Jessen, and Sugden were swarmed at the front of the stage by troops shaking their hands, buying them drinks, asking them where they were from, telling them that we'd played their favorite song. Even the guard was there, handing them beers. I hung back onstage for a few moments, checking and rechecking the gear, an old Satellites habit.

When I stepped down, a soldier came over to me. Like

most everyone in the club, he looked about my age, maybe a little younger. He was tall and gawky, with black hair and an impish grin.

"Boss show, man," he said. "Buy you a beer?"

"Don't drink, but thanks," I said.

"'Roll Over Beethoven'—I dig that song. Reminds me of my girl back home, she always liked to dance to that one. Me, I'm not much of a dancer. But Barb, now, that girl can cut a damn rug."

I smiled. "So where's home?"

"Texas. Small town outside Dallas. Hey, you know any Beatles? I dig 'Ticket to Ride.' That was our prom theme song last year."

"Yeah, we'll be playing that later."

"Great. Thanks. It's so cool that they brought you here. We've had some stupid Korean bands play, but they were really lame. You shoulda heard 'em—they never got the words right, could barely speak English. And they couldn't play too good either."

I laughed. "Well, at least we know the words. Thanks for coming out to see us."

He smiled. "After running supplies up Route Nineteen to Pleiku all week, this is like the royal treatment for us, man."

I thought of Wash. "I know a guy who got transferred to Pleiku. What's it like up there?"

"Hairy, man, like you wouldn't believe. Land mines,

ambushes, snipers. Congs coming at you every which way. We run our convoys and get escorted by gun-trucks, it's so treacherous."

What could I say? I patrolled bars, wrote traffic tickets, and guarded prisoners in hospitals, with the occasional sniper thrown in. Nursery school compared to these guys.

The soldier went on. "So are you all in the military, Special Services or something? Or are you civilians?"

"We're MPs," I said.

The soldier's eyebrows shot up. "No kidding? MPs, they're the ones running the gun-trucks up in Pleiku. They put 'em together themselves. Armor plate a deuce-and-a-half and stick a .50 cal machine gun in the back. We wouldn't be here without 'em."

"That's some serious duty," I said. Real duty. Hardcore duty.

"Well, it's some serious shit going on up there."

I looked at my watch.

"Time for more music," I said. "Good talking to you, man." I shook his hand. "Take care. Hope you enjoy the rest of the show."

"Thanks," the guy said. "And thanks for being here." He sounded like he meant it.

I rounded up the rest of the band and herded them onto the stage. The next two sets went down as well as the first—everybody cheering and clapping and stomping. Then somebody yelled out "Detroit City," the Bobby Bare hit. We knew it, so we played it. It started out well enough, every-one roaring drunk and singing along. But when we hit the chorus, it was like the air blowing out of a balloon. The sol-diers sang with an ache, eyes shining, *"I wanna go home/I wanna go home/Oh, how I wanna go home."*

I looked out over the crowd, wondering what we'd just done.

Cheers to tears in two minutes flat. Now what?

What was it Uncle Roy had told me once, about the band controlling the show? "You can make them happy," he'd said, "you can make them cry, make them beat each other up, or make them go home early. It's all up to you."

Now it was up to us to send these guys back to their barracks feeling as good as they did a song ago. Our last tune had to be a killer.

Jessen must have read my mind. "'96 Tears'!" he hissed at me.

He'd only just figured it out; we'd never practiced it. Could we pull it off? "Are you sure?" I hissed back.

Ben nodded. "They're drunk, what do they know?"

I turned to Sugden. "We're doing '96 Tears.'"

He made a face. "Are you kidding?"

"Look, for you it's a continuous A, you can't go wrong. Then it's an F-sharp minor and a D. I'll cue you."

"Damn." He shook his head. Then he shrugged. "Okay, let's do it."

"What are we doing?" Ioli yelled from behind the drums.

"'96 Tears,'" I told him.

"Excellent!"

Ben launched into the organ intro, Mike snapped the snare hit, and Jon and I joined in. The response was instant.

"*Too many teardrops for one heart to be cryin',*" I sang, and the whole club burst into voice with me. By the last verse everyone was on their feet, some even up on the tables, dancing, clapping, chanting. It was the perfect end to our best show yet.

We packed up our gear, the manager shooed out the stragglers, and we watched as groups of sloshed and beaming soldiers stumbled away from the club, arms around each other's shoulders, voices raised and giggling, "*Let me hear you cry, now, ninety-six tears! Yeah! C'mon now . . . !*"

THE GUN

The place was crowded, scores of medical staff laughing, dancing, drinking. And drinking. And there were loads of pretty nurses around. One in particular reminded me of Judy. Dark hair, terrific face, amazing backside. Drunk.

I found out later that she was a nurse working at the EVAC hospital, so I stopped by on patrol a couple of times. Turned out Nurse Butz was a lieutenant, though, completely out of my league.

I'd been trying not to think about Judy too much lately. I'd written her back, a pretty lame letter about the weather here and the food and the painting I'd been doing around the camp. Some nights before lights-out, I'd tried to sketch Judy from the picture I kept in my duffel. But I could never get it quite right. She never looked the way I remembered her. So I gave up. I hadn't gotten another letter from her.

I had never tried to sketch Lynda. Guess I had never

wanted to. She was like a secret, something you didn't want to commit to paper.

We'd just stepped out of Lyndabar when we got a radio message about a traffic accident nearby, with a possible fatality. We tore to the scene, an intersection with a stop sign, where a U.S. Army step van was turned on its side, a smashed-up ARVN three-quarter-ton next to it.

An ARVN soldier lay faceup in the street. His neck was at a strange tilt. A purple pool was growing around his head. A few GIs stood around.

We jumped out and headed for the man down.

"He's dead," a couple of the soldiers said. "Ran the stop sign."

I'd never touched a dead person before. I'd seen quite a few since coming to Vietnam. But I'd never touched one.

Do it, Kohler. You're an MP.

I knelt down, picked up the ARVN's wrist, and checked for a pulse. Nothing. He was still warm.

His eyes were half closed, as if he were falling asleep. Flies buzzed around his mouth.

He was young: my age. Glossy black hair in a tight crew cut, a cowlick over the forehead.

Did he want to be a soldier?

I groped for the jugular.

Nothing.

I was kneeling next to a dead kid, touching him. I didn't know what I was supposed to feel.

174

So I made sure I didn't feel anything. My face hardened.

I shook my head at Toby.

The driver of the step van, an army soldier, sat on the side of the road, his head in his hands. Blood streamed from a cut on his forehead and a gash across his left palm.

"I killed him, I killed him, I can't believe I killed him," he kept saying over and over, rocking back and forth. Blood dripped between his knees to the dusty red curb.

I wasn't sure if he was upset because the other driver died, or because he thought he was going to get in trouble because the other driver died.

I sat down next to him and tried to calm him down. "Hey, it's okay. It was an accident. He ran the stop sign. That's what's going in our report."

An army ambulance pulled up. The medics ran over.

The soldier stopped muttering but kept rocking. He was shivering.

"It's not your fault, man," Toby told the guy as the medics checked him over. He stopped rocking as they bandaged him up. "It's just one of those things that happens. You're not getting in any trouble. You don't have nothing to worry about."

The medics finished. "He'll be fine," they told us, then raced off in the ambulance. The ARVN MPs arrived and tended to their casualty. We watched as they lifted the soldier into a black plastic body bag. He looked like a life-sized rag doll, limp, limbs hanging. They folded his arms across his chest, then pulled the zipper closed over his face. They loaded the bag into the back of their vehicle and sped away.

"Come on, man, it'll be a kick," Ioli said over lunchtime mystery meat and powdered milk in the mess hall.

Lynda had been pressuring me for weeks to bring her along on one of the Banana gigs. We were playing three or four gigs a week now at clubs all over town and in the surrounding area. Transportation and supply companies, officer parties, other MP installations. And Lynda wanted to come with us. Since Ioli had taken a shine to Angel, one of the Lyndabar girls, now he was pestering to bring them to one of our shows too. It would be totally against the rules. But Lynda could be very . . . persuasive. And now Ioli.

I shook my head.

I knew I shouldn't be seeing Lynda. I should have quit her weeks ago. There was really no point to it, to us. It wasn't like I was in love with her, like I ever could be in love with her. And there was always the risk, that sneaking possibility that maybe Lynda wasn't who she made herself out to be. That maybe the VC had gotten to her, too. So far, though, the army hadn't put the Lyndabar off-limits.

Something about her, something about me, kept me

going back. The way she looked at me, like I was her brave American hero. The way she whispered things, her lips hot and fluttering on my earlobe. The way her body felt, unfolding and winding around mine. It was like I couldn't think. The danger was exciting.

What are you doing? This isn't you, I would hear the voice in my head. But who was I? I wasn't sure I knew anymore. Would I be messing around with a girl like Lynda back home? No. Never. But this wasn't home. Nowhere near it. This was thousands of miles and a lifetime away from all I knew of home. And plenty of guys visited the bar girls. Because maybe that's just what you did in a war.

Ioli leaned over the table and lowered his voice. "Let's do it tonight. We leave here, pick up the girls on the way to the gig, then drop 'em off on the way back. Nobody knows, no big deal."

I turned the idea over in my head as I chewed. If Leadbetter ever found out, it would mean the end of the band, without a doubt. Still, there was something irresistible about the challenge, about trying to pull it off.

"I don't know, man," I said. I put down my fork.

"It'll be easy," Ioli said. "Lyndabar's not too far from the gig." The show was at an army compound right in town. "It's after curfew, so none of our guys'll be downtown. Nobody'll know."

Could we do it? Should we do it?

Ioli waited for my answer as I finished off my milk and

wiped my mouth with the back of my hand.

"Okay," I said, standing up from the table. "Tonight."

No stops. No detours.

Except this once.

We picked up the girls in the three-quarter-ton. Not just Lynda and Angel. Kim and Cheri too. "I did not think you would mind," Lynda said as they climbed up into the truck. They were all done up in their sparkly, high-heeled best, giggly and excited. The guys didn't seem to care.

By the end of the night, Lynda and her girls were completely sloshed. They could barely walk. We helped them out to the truck and told them to stay there while we packed up. We were running back and forth between the club and the truck, breaking down equipment, loading amps, guitars, our PA system. Finally, everything was packed and we were almost ready to leave.

"Hang on," I told everyone at the truck. "I'll be right back."

I ran inside, got the gig money, and grabbed my guitar.

I stepped back outside and froze.

Lynda was standing in front of the door with a .25 automatic in her hand. She was crying, babbling something in Vietnamese. She had the gun trained on me.

Trust no one.

Jesus Christ.

I quickly scanned the area, not moving my head. I didn't see anyone else, just our group. Sugden and Jessen were in the back of the truck, their eyes wide. Ioli was standing near Lynda, his mouth open.

Lynda—had she turned? Was she the enemy?

So this is what it feels like. Face-to-face with a Vietnamese holding a gun. And I'm not even in the jungle.

I reached for my pistol but realized I didn't have it. None of us had weapons. This night, I was just a guy playing guitar on an army base in Vietnam. Sweat stung my eyes and I tried to swallow.

Mike started yelling at Lynda. "I was just kidding! I was just kidding!" He waved his arms, trying to distract her. He looked over at me. "She pulled it out of her pocket, man, I had no idea!" He waved at Lynda again. "Come on, Lynda, I was just kidding!"

Lynda looked like an injured animal, ready to lash out if anyone came near.

"What?!" I hissed to Mike, not moving an inch. I was barely breathing. "You were just kidding about what?!"

The gun bobbled as Lynda sobbed. "You have a nurse girlfriend at EVAC hospital!"

My fear suddenly drained. Exasperation welled in its place.

Nurse Butz. Ioli must've let it slip.

No freaking way. Jealousy? That's what this is all about?

Lynda wasn't VC; she was a woman scorned. I'd thought

I was a goner. And now we could be in some seriously deep shit, lose the band, maybe even face a court-martial. All because Lynda was jealous.

I tried to play it cool. My mouth said, "Lynda, no way, come on, now . . ." But my mind said, *We had girls with us. We went out of our way, made a detour, totally unauthorized. And to top it off, she brought a gun onto the base. The other girls probably have guns too.*

It started to sink in.

Guns on base. That was a *major* offense.

"Mike told me," Lynda sobbed again. Streaks of mascara made a black web on her face. "He told me about the party nurse." Moonlight glinted orange off the jittering gun, which was still pointed at me.

"Kidding! I was just kidding!" Ioli. Somebody needed to shut him up.

I'd had enough. I walked slowly up to Lynda. I knew she wouldn't shoot me. I was the hero, right? I unwrapped her fingers from the gun.

"Everything's okay, that's my girl," I said softly, putting my arm around her and guiding her back to the truck. I slid the gun into my pocket. Then I played the part of consoling boyfriend as she buried her face in my shoulder and wept, murmuring in Vietnamese.

I felt like I was going to explode. I wanted to punch someone.

Lynda was a noodle in my arms, drunk and wobbly. I

lifted her up into the truck and settled her down.

I closed the door and headed around to the driver's side. Ioli was standing next to the truck, looking helpless. "Damn, Dean, I had no idea she'd flip out," he said, following me. "I'm sorry, man."

I wanted to tackle him. How could he be so stupid?

How could you be so stupid, Kohler? You brought her here.

"Shut up and get in," I snarled.

And yet, despite my anger, I couldn't help thinking that I was kind of flattered that Lynda felt that passionately about me.

It turned me on.

Two weeks later, Jessen and I were in the mess hall, grabbing some chow after our day shift with the prisoners out by battalion headquarters. Ioli came in, just off town patrol.

"Hey, did you hear about the jeep that got blown up?"

He set his tray down across from Jessen and me.

We shook our heads. "They had us out in the Valley," I said. "What happened?"

Ioli sat down. "Right in front of a laundry this afternoon." He scooped up a forkful of grayish green beans and shoveled it into his mouth. "Some sergeant from the supply company," he said between chews. "He was inside picking up his stuff, you know? Comes out, and a few miles down the road, *blam!* Jeep and driver blown to bits."

181

"No way," Jessen said, putting down his dry roll. No butter today, as usual. "What was it?"

"Grenade. Local kid. Little, like an eight-year-old. Tossed it into the gas tank." Ioli took a swig of powdered milk.

Trust no one.

My skin tightened. I put down my fork. "So the VC's got the kids working for them now?"

Ioli shrugged and kept eating.

"What about all those kids downtown," Jessen said, "selling us the postcards and the cigarettes and junk?"

"And what about the ones who come here every day," Ioli said, "with the House Mouses, you know?"

I could tell we were all thinking the same thing. That maybe those kids were waiting for the right minute to take out some soldiers. Or blow up the camp. But none of us said it out loud.

I shook my head. "How the hell are you supposed to tell?"

"Don't know, man," Ioli said. "They all look the same to me, you know?"

I thought of Lynda. I was still seeing her, dropping by on patrols when I could. I had just been at the Lyndabar the day before.

My stomach burned.

THE MOUNTAIN

"**H**ey, man, what's going on?"

I slid the amp onto the back of the truck and turned around.

It was those guys. The visitors.

We'd seen them in the mess hall at evening chow, breaking bread with the company. They weren't from the 127th. We weren't exactly sure who they were. Guests of the captain, we just assumed. They'd ridden into Dodge City in an armored jeep. Word was that they'd been out in the thick of the jungle and had been sent into town for supplies or something. They looked pretty young for their rank, though. Nineteen or twenty, like the rest of us—but wearing E-8 stripes. It looked fishy to me. It didn't seem as if they could've been in that long. Ioli thought they must have been battle heroes or something.

We had more important things to worry about. Like tonight's gig.

"Heading up the mountain," I told them as I reached for another amp. "Got a rock band, we're playing an enlisted club up there."

"Cool," one of the guys said. "Mind if we tag along?"

Desolate mountain, the mountain that's always watching us. Deep jungle. At night, Charlie's time. With no weapons—Leadbetter's rules.

Would we mind bringing a jeep with a .50 cal machine gun mounted on top along?

"Not at all," I said, and tossed him an ammo box full of mike cords.

The highway turned to dirt at the base of the mountain. I leaned forward over the steering wheel, straining to see the road in the dark. We climbed and climbed up the ragged mountain, following the winding road. We sliced between giant black trees and tunneled through the damp smell of moss and decaying leaves. Clouds covered the moon. Shadows lunged and lurked. The whole world seemed to end just beyond the headlights. My gut tightened.

Ioli, riding shotgun, turned nervously in his seat. "Those guys are still behind us, right?"

I glanced in the rearview mirror. Two yellow orbs hovered in the distance. "Yeah, I see their headlights."

"Cool. You guys okay?" he yelled out the rear window.

Sugden and Jessen were in back with the equipment, sitting low. "Yeah, we're good," Sugden answered. He was nervous, I could hear it in his voice. He slouched lower in the truck bed.

"Army shoulda put streetlights up here," Jessen said. He folded his arms around himself. "It's dark as hell."

Fog swirled around the truck as we went higher and higher, farther and farther. It spiraled up from the ground, cloaking the dangerous curves. I slowed to a crawl, trying to keep the road in view. Through the mist, branches and leaves shifted. Everything was moving, tangled. Spooky. Charlie's country. Was the enemy out there, watching? Who could know?

"Hell of a place for a military outpost," I mumbled, my heart thumping in my chest.

Ioli gave a halfhearted laugh and checked again that the gun-jeep was behind us.

The fog grew thicker as we climbed.

Ioli leaned out his window. "Looks like we're driving through a damn cloud."

"No kidding," I said. I sat even farther forward, my nose almost to the windshield.

It was hard to make out anything in the wet and the mist, which was like rain without the drops. The vapors seemed to suck us in. The fog swallowed the engine's noise until there was no sound. We traveled on. No moon. No stars. Only the thick silence and murky white.

Is this what it's like to be dead?

The thought came and went in the blink of an eye, and

then we saw coils of concertina wire and a line of sandbag bunkers in the headlights.

Ioli exhaled. "Thank you, God."

We found the club and started loading in. My heart was still racing and I felt like I was moving under water, my fingers fumbling with the cases and cords. I didn't know what it was, but for some reason I couldn't focus. The front half of my mind was getting ready for a gig. But the back half was filled with explosions—ambushes, red fire, and black smoke, people burning and screams and—

Calm, Kohler. The camp is fortified. You're fine. Everything's fine.

I willed my brain to concentrate. I looked around the club. It was pretty nice, decorated with a seascape mural behind the stage. There were a few troops milling around, some wearing just their army T-shirts and fatigue pants.

Sugden took his bass from its case and noticed me staring at the guys. "Couldn't get away with that at Dodge City."

"Guess when you're sitting in Charlie's front yard, uniform protocol's not a huge priority," I said. I tried to plug a cord into my guitar.

Sugden put a hand on my shoulder. "The drive shake you up?" he asked quietly.

I wanted to nod. I wanted to say "Yes" and "I'm scared."

I shrugged instead.

Sugden stared at me for a second. He understood. I could see it in his eyes. He gave my shoulder a squeeze.

Then he headed for the bar.

I watched as he joined Jessen, Ioli, and the guys from the gun-jeep. A soldier leaning on the bar next to them nodded at me. There was something about him, about the others from the camp. They all had the same look. Dark shadows under the eyes. A weariness. A heaviness. Even their smiles seemed solemn.

These guys have seen the Deep Serious.

A big guy came out from a back room. He was wearing a top hat, black, velvet. Not like a magician. More like the Mad Hatter.

It was the most ridiculous hat I'd ever seen. So unexpected. So unregulation. So totally preposterous. It made me laugh out loud, and I decided then and there that I had to have it. I *needed* that damn hat. I made my way over to the bar.

"So here's the Electrical Banana!" Mad Hatter pumped each of our hands. "Glad to see you. We weren't sure you were gonna make it."

That makes about seven of us, brother.

"Took us a while to get through the fog," I said.

"Nice place you got here," Jessen added.

"I'm Lomax, the club manager. Anything you need, just ask. Give you a hand with your stuff?"

"No, thanks, man," I said. "We got it."

Nice guy.

I hoped he'd sell me his ridiculous hat after the show.

* * *

Drums pounded.

Guitar snarled, the five-note riff a battering ram.

Keys-soaked chords primitive, lyrics simple.

Bass throb built to the rip-roaring chorus.

And a tribe of battle-worn warriors roared along:

You really got me

You really got me

You really got me

I looked out over the crowd. Fists waved in unison, tired eyes lifted. I turned to the band. Sugden's head was bowed over his bass, nodding to the rhythm. Jessen swayed, trancelike, behind the organ. Ioli beat his drums, mouth open, grinning, sweat flying with every blow.

Two and a half minutes of pure freedom, courtesy of the Kinks.

The band was no longer a hobby, a my-summer-in-Vietnam science project. No longer something I was doing just because I happened to know how.

I knew that it was monumental. Huge. To me. To the band guys. To the soldiers we played for.

One thing was for sure:

It was a ticket out of there. Away from guns and explosions and fear. Fear that you couldn't admit to because you were a tough, strong American soldier. Fear that you couldn't talk about or it would all come crashing down on you.

It was a way out—if only for three sets.

25

THE TOP HAT

We were packing up, moving in the I-love-you-man bliss of the best gig we'd ever played. Better than any of the downtown shows, it blew the 127th gig right out of the freaking water. It was as if these guys never got any entertainment way up on the mountain. Like the army had forgotten about them. They swarmed us after the show, slapping our backs and chattering about the music and breaking into drunken song and dance. And they kept the bartender busy buying beer after beer for the band.

Maybe a few too many for Sugden. He was taking an awfully long time to load up his gear.

"Sug, pack up your bass, man!" I shouted. Ioli and Jessen headed out the door, equipment under their arms. "We're almost ready to go!"

"Hold your damn horses, I'm coming!" he yelled back. He strolled out of the back room, the top hat on his head, a foot-long cigarette holder in his hand. In his yellow Banana suit, he looked like some British dandy gone psychedelically wrong.

Sugden gave the velvet brim an adoring stroke. "I told Lomax I liked it," he said slowly, slurring, "and he said I could have it. And look, he gave me a cigarette holder too."

"Yeah, beautiful," I said, snapping the locks shut on my guitar case. I pointed to his bass leaning on the wall. "You mind packing up your gear so we can hit the road?"

Outside in the mountain fog, Ioli and Jessen had the truck nearly loaded. They were talking with the visitors, who were waiting for us in their armored jeep. By the light of their headlamps, I swung my guitar into the truck, then dashed back into the club to get paid. Inside, Sugden was moving at half speed, taking forever to wipe down his guitar.

"Jesus, give me that." I grabbed the bass, stowed it in the case, and gave him a gentle shove toward the door. "Come on, let's go, everyone's waiting for us."

Outside, Ioli, Jessen, and I changed back into our fatigues—Leadbetter's rules. Sugden strolled around the truck like he was the Duke of York, saying, "Mind the gap!" and "Cheeri-o" in a mock English accent, waving the cigarette holder around. He was still in his Banana clothes. The visitors cracked up, egging him on.

Ioli and I climbed into the truck's cab and Jessen hopped in back with the equipment. We were all sapped, rack ops definitely on our minds.

"Hey, Prince Albert in the can," Ioli shouted, "you wanna get into your uniform, Your Highness?"

Sugden doffed his hat, bowed deeply, and nearly toppled over. Then he leaned on the front bumper, adjusting the hat just so on his head.

"Sug, we're leaving!" Jessen yelled. I started up the truck. The visitors started up the jeep. Engines rumbled.

Sugden took the hint. Slowly, he unbuttoned his yellow trousers. They fell to the ground. He struggled for balance, hopping around as he tried to free his feet.

Jessen sighed from the back. "Looks like we're gonna be here all night."

"I know what'll hurry his ass up." I hit the headlights.

The blinding glare didn't even faze him. Sug danced a little soft-shoe in the spotlight, clad only in boots, boxers, Banana shirt, and the top hat. Then he stepped up on the bumper, sat down on the hood, and crossed his legs. He took a drag from the cigarette holder and blew lazy smoke rings over his head. They merged with the fog and disappeared.

"For crying out loud." I groaned. "Looks like he needs a little more persuading."

I gave the truck some gas. It inched forward, Sugden still perched on the hood. I waited for him to tell me to stop. For him to hop off and get dressed so we could get going. But he just sat there.

I opened the truck up a bit more. The guys in the jeep followed. Now we were moving at a pretty good clip through the jungle. And Sugden was still sitting on the hood. Soon we were flying through the dark, our yellow-shirted, pantsless hood ornament apparently enjoying the view.

And then the jungle exploded in noise and smoke.

Everything went slow-motion. Automatic-weapons fire rattled off to our right. Muzzle flashes sparked in the fog like lightning bolts from the ground.

It sounded like three shooters at least, maybe more. Bullets came from the bushes, from the trees. Plumes of dirt geysered up next to the truck. Branches tumbled from the sky. Leaves rained down on the windshield, over Sugden, who sat frozen on the hood.

Sugden . . .

"Holy shit!" Jessen yelped and dived for the floor in back.

"Get down! Get down!" the boys in the jeep yelled. They opened up the machine gun, ripping into vines and low canopy, mowing down the vegetation. Trees disintegrated under the .50 cal's firepower. It looked like someone was swinging a giant machete through the jungle.

Everything was noise—a metallic, deafening clatter that slashed at my ears. I could hear bullets tearing through the shrubbery, the *zing!* of rounds grazing the jeep behind us. I ducked as low as I could in the driver's seat, my foot still on the gas pedal, sweat pouring from my body. The sharp smell of gunpowder burned my nostrils.

Please, not Sugden . . .

Ioli reached down behind him and pulled out a "grease gun," an M3 handheld machine gun. It was half the length of a Thompson, with a clip at the bottom, like in all the John Wayne movies. Definitely not MP issue. I watched openmouthed as he stuck the muzzle out the window and squeezed off fire into the chaos.

Jessen kept low, scrambling for his pot and flak jacket. I looked in front of me, eyes peering just over the dashboard. The truck was still moving. I was still driving.

And Sugden was still sitting on the hood.

I've got to get us out of here. Please, let me get us out of here.

The MP training kicked in.

Drive out of an ambush.

Everything went fast-motion. I punched the gas pedal, fighting for control of the truck, jouncing for traction on the dirt road.

Please, God, don't let Sugden get hit, don't let him fall off, please, God . . .

"Come on, you freakin' scumbags! Come and get some of this!" Ioli bellowed as he fired out the window.

"Where the hell'd you get that?" I yelled to him as I clutched the steering wheel, struggling to see the ground ahead of me.

"From the guys in the jeep!" he shouted back. "They said

we could have it in case we needed it!"

And then it was over.

It had seemed like hours—it probably only took minutes—for the noise and smoke and whizzing bullets to fade away.

I tried to swallow, but the sides of my throat stuck together. I couldn't take my foot off the gas pedal.

Keep going. What if there's more?

We had to get Sugden into the truck. I eased on the brakes and slowed to a halt. I could see the jeep's headlights pull up behind me. My lungs loosened just a hair.

Sugden had had enough. He jumped off the hood, a silhouette, still smoking his cigarette.

Jessen was belly-down in the back, his eyes wide, his jaw clenched. Ioli was gripping the M3 out the window, sweat gleaming on his face.

Sugden climbed up into the truck bed with Jessen. He flicked an ash over the side.

"Chin up, chaps," he said.

Nobody said a word as we made our way down the mountain.

"Should we tell Captain?"

Jessen had his head poked inside the rear window. Sugden sat next to him in the back of the truck, mute, expressionless. I glanced back at Jon every few minutes in the mirror. I couldn't tell if he was okay.

"No way," I said, trying to keep my eye on the road too. "If he knows we were ambushed, he'll never let us go on gigs anymore."

Ioli gave a nervous sort of half laugh, half snort. "Yeah, I guess if any of us had gotten waxed tonight, Captain would have a tough time explaining what we were doing up on the mountain in an army truck full of instruments."

"No kidding," I said. "He'd be in a world of trouble, letting us use a military vehicle for our own personal business. If he knew that this band thing was actually kind of dangerous—"

"Kind of?" Jessen squeaked. He jerked a thumb at the headlights of the gun-jeep. "If they hadn't been following behind us with their .50 cal, we never would've made it out of there alive!"

The ambush replayed in my mind, an endless loop of red sparks in the fog, machine-gun spray, branches flying, the jungle coming apart.

We might not have made it. Was the band worth it?

Ioli spoke up. "Hey, you guys think we shouldn't do the Banana anymore?"

I knew what my answer would be. The only answer it could be. But I wanted to hear it from the band.

No one said anything. Then a voice came from the back of the truck.

"Hell, no!" Sugden stuck his head through the window. In the rearview, I could see he had the top hat clenched in his hand. "No way we're quitting the Banana. No freaking way."

Ioli grinned. "Well, guess that settles that."

As we pulled into Dodge City, we decided not to breathe a word of the ambush to anyone. The guys in the gun-jeep agreed to keep quiet about it too. Silently, we unloaded our gear and dropped into our bunks.

The next morning we headed to the shower. We filed past the row of barracks, zipper bags with soap and wash-cloths in our hands, plastic shower shoes on our feet. Ioli, Jessen, and I had towels around our waists.

Sugden wore only the top hat.

THE TRANSFER

"Looks like I'm out of the band," Sugden said, falling into a chair at dinner mess a week later.

I swallowed my meat loaf. "What are you talking about? You don't seem so good, man."

Sugden looked me straight in the eyes and I saw it. He was scared. "The transfer list," he said. "I'm on it. Pleiku."

Pleiku.

He'd heard the same things I had about Pleiku. We all had, playing in the band. Every transportation company we'd visited, every soldier who'd made the drive, the story was always the same. Blown bridges, ambushes, land mines, rockets, grenades, snipers, near misses, direct hits—night and day, day in and day out.

Sug was on edge. A few days ago, he and Voina were escorting a convoy through town when the oil tanks at the depot lit up like a volcano. Seventeen vehicles—and their

197

army personnel—had vanished in a giant fireball in front of him. The mop-up ops were the ugliest we'd seen.

"You sure?" It was a stupid question. Of course he was sure.

"They posted it," he said, blinking behind his glasses. He lit up a smoke. "I saw it. I'm going." He stared down at the table.

"Is this because of what happened a week ago?" I asked, still not believing what I was hearing. "On the mountain?"

The visitors, the guys in the gun-jeep, had left the camp before we'd even made it to formation. They hadn't said a word to anyone; they'd just disappeared.

"You think those guys told Leadbetter?" I wondered aloud.

Sugden shrugged. "I don't know, man. The transfer's just up there on the board. It was probably in the works for weeks."

My insides felt like they were sinking. What about the band? We couldn't have the Banana without Jon. He'd been with us from the beginning. He was my best friend here. We had been inseparable for nearly a year, stumbling through training and now trying to figure out this weird and dangerous country. And what about me? If something happened to Jon, if there was no band, I wasn't sure I could . . .

No. He can't go.

I stood up and grabbed my empty tray. "I've got to go talk to somebody."

"You're up to something, Kohler," Sugden said. "Forget about it, man. They've already cut the orders at Battalion."

"Yeah," I called behind me, "we'll see."

I hunted down Sergeant Hall at the Longbranch, playing cards with some of the other officers. He listened to me, then shook his head. "They're running short of bodies up in Pleiku; they need soldiers. If the orders have been cut, it's too late now to change anything," he said.

Why were they running short of troops? WIA—wounded in action? KIA—killed in action?

My neck prickled. No. I wasn't going to let it happen. Not to Sug. If Hall couldn't help me, I'd find somebody who could. I went searching for Leadbetter.

I found him outside his quarters. He stood alone, puffing on his pipe, watching the sun go down.

"Sir?"

He turned around, the sky dying red behind him. "What is it, Kohler?"

I explained the situation. How the Banana, our band—his band—was going to lose its bass player. How there could be no band without Jon. I left out the rest. I had a feeling he already knew.

He listened carefully, then frowned. "I'll see what I can do," was all he said when I was through.

"Thank you, sir."

I left him pondering the darkening mountains.

I didn't sleep much that night. Neither did Sugden, tossing and turning above me. The next morning on the way to formation I saw Sug at the bulletin board. As I walked up, he gave me a weird look.

"What?" I said.

"How'd you do that?"

"Do what?"

He pointed to the list.

His name wasn't there.

Pridden, one of the Fucking New Guys, was going instead.

I felt bad for Pridden. But I couldn't stop the small voice inside me that kept saying, *I'm glad it's not Sug.*

Sergeant Hall stuck his head in the barracks door. "Kohler, Sugden. Captain wants you at his jeep in fifteen." And then he was gone.

Jon and I looked at each other across the table where we were cleaning our weapons. I had that sinking feeling you get when you've just been called to the principal's office.

"Sounds serious," said Driscoll, heading out the door for formation.

"Lupica." I sighed as I reassembled my M14. "He finally gave me up."

Jessen put down his *Hit Parader* and sat up in his bunk. "After all this time? No way, it's been weeks. I bet Captain found out about the ambush on the mountain."

Sugden tamped out his cigarette in an empty Coke

can. He looked pale. "Maybe it's about my orders getting changed. Maybe they're sending me to Pleiku after all."

I placed my rifle back in the rack. "Only one way to find out."

Leadbetter and his driver were waiting for us at the motor pool, sitting in the jeep. When we first got to Dodge City, he wanted Snuffy Smith on the rim cover of the spare tire. So I'd painted ol' Snuff holding a frothy mug of beer, along with COMMANDING OFFICER, 127TH MP COMPANY stenciled in white letters.

Captain motioned to the backseat. "Get in," he barked, his eyes unreadable behind dark glasses.

Sugden and I climbed in. I noticed Sugden wiping his hands on his fatigues.

The driver swung out onto the highway. Looked like we were headed to the Valley. Leadbetter swiveled in his seat to face us.

He frowned. "Men, we've got a problem."

Oh, man. Here it comes. It's got to be something big if he's stealing us away to tell us.

Sugden stared blankly at Captain. "The fuel depot bombing," Captain said, "that's hit the company pretty hard. Has everybody shaken up."

Yeah, you could say.

The ARVN had caught the bombers. They were VC who'd come up from the water in sampans. Everyone at Dodge City had been happy to hear the news that the men

201

who'd blown up the convoy and murdered our fellow GIs had been captured. Like everybody else, I wanted nothing more than to get even with the bombers for what they'd done.

The ARVN shot the bombers through the head a few days later at a public execution at the soccer field downtown. We'd been warned that morning at the briefing that we'd be hearing gunfire at noon. All the MPs on patrol parked outside the stadium. It looked like the whole city was inside, a sea of Vietnamese. We could hear the people cheering and shouting like there was a game going on, like it was home-versus-away in the big season-ender. I could feel myself getting caught up in the scene, everyone panting for blood.

And at 1200 we heard the shots. Seven of them. The sound rang through the stadium and echoed off the plaster buildings outside. A giant roar went up from the crowd—victorious—like their team had just scored the winning goal.

There was no trial, no due process or whatever. Just payback, no questions asked.

Seven more lives ended. Do you feel better?

Now death was a spectator sport.

Hearing those shots and cheers made it start coming together that day. The snipers, the explosions, the ambush, the executions, the killings and death and utter waste of human life. They were like links on a chain that weighed on my neck, digging and pressing into me, until it was becoming a part of me. I didn't want it. I couldn't make it stop. The only time I didn't feel it was when I was playing with the band.

"It ain't fun and games out here anymore," Captain was saying. "I know it, you know it, the company knows it."

The ambush on the mountain. Does he know? Did he find out?

"Things are heating up," Captain went on. "And I'm not talking about the weather."

Where is this leading? It can't be good.

I glanced over at Sugden. He had his hands in his lap now, clenched tight.

Captain gazed up into the green mountainside whizzing beside the jeep. He was so intent, he looked like he was flushing Charlie from the trees with his eyes. Then he turned back toward us.

"I need the company focused. At its best. I need the 127th coming together as a unit, a team. A family. We're all working hard out there. The enemy's keeping us on our toes. But we need a little R & R for the brain, a little camaraderie. So I want you guys playing for the company again. ASAP. Am I understood?"

That's it?

No Lupica UA report? No mountain ambush? No Sugden transfer?

Sugden's face was still a blank.

I fought back a grin. "Yes, sir. You name the date."

The driver pulled up in front of the PX at Battalion Headquarters.

"Excellent," Leadbetter said. "Sergeant Hall will let you know. Now"—Captain jumped out—"we've got a reel-to-reel to buy. This way, men."

After much consideration, and on our recommendation, Captain chose an Akai M8 for his tape-listening and recording pleasure.

I felt as if the Banana had just dodged a bullet.

127TH, AGAIN

Lynda pressed her body against me, kissing me, long, wet, slow. I knew if I didn't get out of there we'd be starting all over again. Plus, Leach was picking me up out front in a couple of minutes.

I didn't really even know what I was doing. I'd spent the night again. I was pushing my luck, I knew. But I couldn't keep away.

It was like a craving. Not for Lynda, really, though the things she did to my body had every nerve ending begging for more. It was more like a compulsion. Sneaking off to the Lyndabar, sneaking back into camp. Could I pull it off? Could I beat the risk?

"I've got to go," I said, reaching for the door.

"Are you sure?" she whispered, running her tongue over my ear.

"Yeah," I said, disentangling myself from her arms.

"I'll see you soon."

"Wait." She moved to a small dresser and pulled something from the top drawer.

She kissed me again and as I turned to leave she pressed a small photo of herself into my hand.

Leach pulled up as I was reading what was written on the back. *Forget me not, Lynda*. Like we were boyfriend and girlfriend. Like we were together. Like this was serious.

Like she was Judy.

I had the sudden urge to run.

In Nam, second time's a charm, I guess. Or maybe keeping your ass from getting sniped or blown up has a way of bringing folks together.

Three weeks later the whole company turned out. Captain had chosen September 4, Labor Day, for our gig. He wanted a big blowout party—food, drinks, music. Soldiers were packed wall to wall inside the Longbranch, the rest spilling over outside to the tables and chairs and striped patio umbrellas Leadbetter had appropriated for us from somewhere.

We had them from the first chord. We could tell. We'd been playing for so long now—three months, four gigs a week—that we knew when a crowd was with us. First it was the heads nodding along to the beat. Then it was the smiles of recognition as we ripped into everybody's favorite songs. Then it was always the bodies moving, the clapping, the shouting for more. Guys got happy and they wanted you to know about it.

The soldiers of the 127th were digging it. Really digging it. Granted, we were a lot better than the first time around. Jessen and Ioli were singing backup now. We were polished. A music machine. We sounded an awful lot like the Satellites, actually.

The company was having a blast. Even Lupica and his boys were cheering. Everybody was loose, and by the third set the band and I were playing it by ear. "California Sun," "Louie, Louie," "Satisfaction," "I'm Free," "Long Tall Sally," "Run for Your Life," "You Don't Need a Reason." Guys were yelling "Banana, number one!" Voina shouted, "Elvis!" so I did a verse of "Treat Me Nice." Somebody requested Sonny Bono, so I did an "I Got You Babe" impression. The guys roared.

McClory was more vocal than usual. During a break he teased, "Got an extra spring in your step, Kohler. I wonder why?" He flashed a knowing grin. McClory had been working the front gate the night before, when I'd snuck in from Lynda's. I smirked back at him. "Don't worry, I ain't talking," he said, like a partner-in-crime, and headed for the bar.

After our third set, Leadbetter called me over to his table and introduced me to a friend of his, Captain Needham.

"You've got a great band here," Needham said, returning my salute. His face was craggy, battle hardened. Like a piece of granite.

"Kohler, how about you and the band play for Captain Needham's men?" Leadbetter asked.

"Sure, no problem," I said. "Our pleasure."

"Excellent," Needham said. "My guys could really use some entertainment."

"Where are you located, sir?" I asked.

"Captain Needham's the commanding officer of the MP unit up in Pleiku," Leadbetter said.

Oh.

"Pleiku?" I didn't recognize my own voice.

Leadbetter nodded. "That's right."

Surely, Leadbetter knew about Pleiku, about how dangerous it was. I was stunned he'd even suggest it. We'd never heard from Pridden again after he got transferred up there. We hadn't known him well; he'd only been with the 127th for a couple of weeks. But he'd stopped by our practices a few times and seemed like a nice guy, maybe a little fragile. Most of the FNGs were, at the beginning. I wondered if he was still alive.

Captain sensed my hesitation. "Is there a problem, Kohler?"

Get a grip, Dean, get a grip.

"I don't know, sir," I said, trying to sound in control. "I hear it gets pretty hairy on Highway Nineteen. And, you know, we're not allowed to bring weapons with us." I paused for a moment. I thought of Pridden, thought of Wash up in the mountains, in the jungle. Remote, isolated—go ahead

208

and say it—terrified. In the heat of it. The real thing. And here we were, drinking beer under striped umbrellas like it was a holiday at the beach. Guilt tugged at me.

Did we really want to go up there?

No way. Don't be a hero, my brain screamed.

Heart told brain to shut the hell up.

Yes. They need us. We have to go.

I had an idea. It was probably out of the question. But it was worth a try. "Any chance of a helicopter transport?" I asked.

The captains looked at each other, surprised.

Needham pulled out a half-smoked cigar. Then he nodded his head. "Yeah, I can make that happen. I can send a chopper to come get you men."

"Sure," Leadbetter said. "Good thinking, Kohler. Let's do it. I'll have Sergeant Hall write up the paperwork."

"Excellent," Needham said, shaking my hand. "Kohler, we'll see you in Pleiku real soon."

Pleiku . . .

I turned to leave. I felt like I was breathing water.

I tried not to choke.

I lay back in my bunk, my mind a big, black hole.

Smokey Porter was dead.

He was killed here in Nam last month. My first friend from home to die.

When I was sixteen, I spent a lot of time with Smokey's

dad, Pete Porter, the auto painter at McLean Pontiac. Almost every day after school I'd help him sand the cars. He painted my '56 Pontiac for free for helping him. Smokey was usually there too, until he enlisted. He was sure that if he joined the army instead of waiting to be drafted, he wouldn't get sent to Vietnam. Didn't work out that way. Smokey married Bonnie Jordan from school, a pretty blonde, before he was sent over.

Mom mailed me the newspaper clipping. I read it again, trying to understand.

> *In August 1967, Porter lost his life while heroically leading his squad in defense of a fire support base near An Loc.*
>
> *The citation accompanying the medal read in part:*
>
> *"Disregarding the heavy volleys of fire directed at his company's sector of the perimeter, Sgt. Porter moved across exposed terrain to deploy his men into the most advantageous positions along the line."*

Smokey's life was over. But I was still alive. He was a hero. A real hero. And he was dead.

Why him?

Why not me?

Why am I still here?

I felt like I should cry for him. But the tears didn't come. Just a stone—cold and hard—sitting at the back of my throat. I wanted to cry for myself, because I knew I wasn't myself anymore. I was so tired of feeling that I'd finally stopped feeling at all.

Smokey Porter was never coming back, and his family got a lump of bronze.

I thought about my family. What if I never came back? I imagined Mom, folding up the telegram and tucking it away in the back of her jewelry box with our birth certificates. Mary, sneaking into my bedroom to flip through my record albums because Mom would keep the door closed for the rest of her days. Roy, carefully wiping down my Gretsch, packing it away for good, never to be played again.

And what about Dad? What would he think? Would he remember me proudly?

TDY

"**C**an you guys believe how fast Hall got the paperwork turned around?" Ioli pulled his bass drum out the barracks door. "Drums of destruction comin' at ya," he cracked.

Sergeant Hall had gotten Leadbetter's TDY—Temporary Duty—request through the system in just under three weeks. We were now officially on our way to Pleiku.

I set my amp down on the pallet sidewalk and swiped at the sweat rolling down the back of my neck. "He must really want to get rid of us," I joked. I hoped it was a joke.

"But just for the weekend," Jessen said, giving me a mock slap to the head with his free hand, a whorl of cords in the other. "We'll be back before he even knows we left."

The Electrical Banana was loading out as if it were any other gig, the four of us joking and messing with one another. But we were dancing around what we all didn't want to talk about. We were headed for the hot zone. The jungle. The front line.

At the Labor Day gig, when I'd told the band about Leadbetter wanting us to play for Captain Needham, they'd all kind of shrunk at first. "Think about it," I said as we were packing up our gear. "I already agreed to it. I sort of had to. But if you guys really don't want to do it, I'll go back to Captain and tell him. Of course, he'd probably order us to go anyway."

Sugden said, "I don't have to think about it, man. I'm in." Then Ioli agreed, then Jessen.

"We're the Banana," Ben had said. "It's what we do."

Now, outside of our barracks, Sugden sat cross-legged on his bass amp and lit up a cigarette. "First time one of our gigs has ever been army-authorized."

"First time for a chaperone, too," I said. I leaned my guitar case on my amp. "Sergeant Dirks is cool, though. He's been around."

Jessen set the organ in its case next to us. "Dean, you got those TDY papers?"

"Right here." I tapped the envelope in my shirt pocket.

Sugden flicked an ash. "Let me see."

I tossed him the envelope. He unfolded the papers and read. "From Headquarters, Ninety-third Military Police Battalion, San Francisco. Temporary duty to Pleiku, Republic of Vietnam and return to Qui Nhon, Republic of Vietnam. Period of approximately two days. Purpose: Official duty."

Ioli did a little dance, his arms in the air. "Official duty. That's right. Rockin' in the jungle."

"Special instructions: Travel by government vehicle authorized."

"Finally," I grumbled, kneeling to check the microphone box.

"Authorized to carry weapons."

Everyone went quiet.

These weren't Leadbetter's rules.

It became crystal clear. This definitely wasn't an army doctor's party or a gig at the officers' club. This was serious. Officially serious.

Ioli let out a low whistle. "Guess even HQ in San Fran knows what's going on."

We continued loading the equipment out of the barracks in silence.

When we were almost done, Dirks and Leadbetter walked up.

"Men, there's been a change of plans," Captain said, returning our sweaty salutes.

"Sir?" I asked.

He pulled off his sunglasses and squinted at us. "No helos today. Charlie's got air support all tied up. Seems it's a busy day in the jungle."

"We're going some other time, then?" I asked.

"Better start moving this stuff back in." Sugden grabbed an amp.

Leadbetter put a hand on his shoulder. "Hold up there, soldier. You men have got to go today. TDY orders have been issued. They're official; we can't change them. Plus, I promised Captain Needham that you'd come play for his men. And I'm nothing if not a man of my word."

The band exchanged uneasy glances as Captain went on.

"You won't be flying to Pleiku this afternoon. You'll be driving."

My stomach dropped.

"Dirks here knows the way—he's made the trip before. It's a long drive. You can have a deuce-and-a-half."

I swallowed hard. "Drive, sir?" My throat felt dry and my words came out squeaky.

"I'm afraid there's no other way," Captain said, folding and unfolding his glasses. "And I want you to know it could get dangerous. You're already authorized to bring your weapons. All of you are well trained, you're intelligent, and I'm trusting you to use your weapons wisely."

He put his sunglasses back on. "You be careful out there, men. Good luck, and we'll see you when you get back."

Then he went around to each one of us, calling us by our first names and shaking our hands long and hard. In the whole year that we'd known him, it was the first time he'd ever done anything like that.

It reminded me of my dad, seeing me off to war.

* * *

Heading northwest on QL One-Niner, the village-dotted valleys turned to rolling hills and then mountains, creased and green against a brilliant blue sky. Elephant grass as tall as I was shimmied in the hot breeze. Thick mats of trees, their graying branches gnarled and twisted, draped the mountain faces. The lush beauty of the landscape caught me off guard. It was hard to believe that this was a killing zone.

The road was paved but rough and dusty. Our equipment bounced on mattresses in the back of the truck, hidden from the sun under the olive-drab canvas canopy. Sergeant and I were in the cab, Dirks at the wheel. Ioli and Sugden were sitting in the back, looking out the canopy's open back flap. Jessen was standing behind the cab, his head poked up over the canopy's front flap.

"Damn, this thing is heavy," Jessen said, adjusting his flak jacket. We were all wearing them, plus our steel pots. Dirks had told us to put them on and keep them on. "Hot as hell, too."

A series of creeks and rivers tangled through the land. Nearly every bridge we came to was army-temporary, the original reduced to piles of rubble along the riverbed.

"Looks like the Congs have been keeping engineering busy," Dirks said with a dry chuckle. I wondered how he could be so calm. "Get one bridge fixed, they're blowing up another."

As we climbed higher and higher, the road twisted and

turned, winding through deep cuts in the mountains. My stomach started to clench and didn't let go. Prime ambush sites were everywhere. The tall grass grew right up to the side of the road; if a sniper went to work, there'd be no way of telling where the shots were coming from. The tree-covered ridges above one side of the road were perfect places to lob grenades or launch mortars from. And there'd be no escape. If we veered off the pavement, we'd roll straight down the sheer face on the other side.

I shifted uneasily and glanced at the other guys. They were riveted to the open back flap, scanning the landscape. I hoped Dirks knew what he was doing.

"See that?" Dirks said after a while, pointing to a bald spot on a bluff ahead of us. No trees, no shrubs, not a single blade of grass. Just red dust, cratered and desolate. "Agent Orange. Defoliant. Strips it bare. Ain't no hiding up there."

"Looks like the freakin' desert," Ioli said.

"Like the moon," I said.

My ears popped as we made our way onward and upward. I swallowed hard. It didn't help.

"What's that?" Jessen pointed.

A chunk of an army truck, a deuce-and-a-half, just like ours, sat on the side of the road. It was the rear axle, plus the bed, or what was left of it anyway. Charred, with rust the color of blood, it looked like a wounded animal, some sort of weird sacrifice. Scraps of tire tread were scattered nearby.

"Not cool," Jessen mumbled as we rolled on.

My mouth was dry. I took a swig of Kool-Aid from my canteen. It didn't help.

I was scared, but I didn't want to think about it.

"Hold tight," Dirks said after another mile. "Here comes the Hairpin."

We leaned into one another as Dirks rounded the snug U, narrow enough for only a single vehicle.

"What the hell?" Sergeant locked up the brakes.

In front of our vehicle, a pillar of four armored jeeps rocketed straight for us, their M60 machine guns manned, windshields glinting. We could just make out the white stars on the doors—friendlies, army.

"I hope they see us," I blurted. They didn't seem to be slowing. "There's nowhere for us to move but down."

"A long way down," Ioli added.

At the very last moment, the jeeps skidded to a stop in front of us, their tires smoking.

Dirks jumped out and dashed over to the lead jeep. He exchanged a few words with the driver, then climbed back in wearing a smile. "Relax, gentlemen, our escort has arrived."

"Escort?" Ioli asked. "Like a convoy?"

Dirks nodded as he checked and rechecked his rifle. "Seems things have been jumpin' up here the last few days. He says it's been quiet so far today. They're Roadrunners, B Company, 504th MP Battalion. Highway patrol. He said they swept the road for mines first thing this morning, but they want to bring us into Pleiku, just in case."

"Mines?" I didn't know why I was surprised. Hadn't we heard over and over what to expect? But talk was one thing. Being there was different.

"Escort sounds good to me." Sugden slouched lower under the canopy.

The Roadrunners backed up a bit and let us through.

We fell in, two jeeps in front, two behind.

THE PASS

The mountains swallowed us and we kept climbing. And climbing. The road was steep and narrow, the going slow. The machine-gunners in front and in back of us kept their sights trained on the tree lines above.

I wondered what a rocket attack felt like, how a mine blast sounded. Would it hurt? Would I see it? Would I know?

How does it feel to die?

Finally, we reached the summit.

"Mang Yang Pass," Dirks said. "'Ambush Alley.' See over there?" He pointed at a mountainside to the north. Impossibly green grass rippled across its face. But there was something else. White dots. Hundreds of them. In rows. Like a giant game of checkers.

"What are those?" I asked.

"Graves. French. The Viets kicked the living crap out

of the French up here in the fifties, First Indochina War. French buried their KIAs right over there, upright and facing west."

"Damn French, always dramatic," Sugden said, huddled into himself.

I fought off a shiver and hugged my rifle more tightly.

Then we were rolling downhill, past dust-caked carcasses of burned-out vehicles—trucks, jeeps, a tank. Metal skeletons scattered across barren cliffs, full of holes. The land was desolate, pocked and cratered. Shadows settled into the hollows.

It was like driving through a nightmare.

"Man, they don't mess around up here," Jessen said, then fell silent like the rest of us.

Thank you, Captain, for weapons.

We heard something from behind. It was a low thudding, getting closer, louder. The air, heavy and red in the dying sunlight, shuddered around the truck. A column of UH-1s, Huey gunships, banked in low over us, their *thut-thut-thut* so thundering, so powerful, our chests vibrated. The rotor wash lashed at the truck canopy. For an instant, we could see the faces of the door gunners, standing out on the rocket pods, M60s at the ready. I made eye contact with one. His head was thrown back, his mouth open wide— Laughing? Screaming?—his eyes wild. He waved—Hello? Good-bye?—as the choppers swooped up and out over the ridgeline in front of us.

Moments later we heard the unmistakable clatter of machine guns strafing a mountainside nearby and the echoing explosions of air-to-ground rockets.

"Sweet Jesus." My heart hammered against my rib cage. "Keep rolling, Sergeant."

Oh, God, keep rolling.

Then I saw it.

I wasn't sure what it was, at first.

I squinted at it. It was skewered atop a bamboo pole stuck in the dust. It looked like a withered pumpkin. Round, leathery. A deep orangish brown. Except the pumpkin had hair. Black hair. And teeth, sitting crooked in a gaping hole that used to be a mouth, but now it was filled with flies. Green flies buzzed from the mouth to a pair of holes— sunken, empty—where eyes once were. The eye holes were nearly sitting on top of the mouth hole, the dangling flap that was once a nose had folded under.

My throat closed. I couldn't breathe.

I turned away and looked around the truck. Sugden's face was a stone wall. Jessen's eyes were squeezed shut. Ioli was kneading his brows, staring down at the truck bed, rhythmically clenching his rifle with his other hand.

I made a gagging noise. I pressed my hand to my mouth.

"Oh, yeah, that," Dirks said as calmly as if we'd just driven past a bus stop. "Guess I should've warned you. Korean Tigers, they like to send the Congs a message. Loud

and clear. The Roadrunners, they figure the road signs can't hurt, so they leave 'em up there. 'Here today, gone to Maui.'"
He laughed.

My stomach was in my mouth. My brain was erupting, horror from deep down inside strangling me.

What the hell kind of place is this?

I squeezed my eyes shut, watching red and white explosions behind my lids.

I don't belong here.

We don't belong here.

Please, God, what the hell are we doing here?

I opened my eyes and looked to the sky. White clouds billowed against dazzling blue. The mountains soared, ancient and green.

We passed four more heads.

Dirks followed the lead gun-jeeps as they turned off onto a dirt trail. The jungle pressed in on us, branches slapping at the doors, the wet, earthy smell of decay filling our noses. We leaned forward in our seats, fingers on the rifles' safeties. Deeper and deeper we rolled, mile after mile, the sun vanishing from our tunnel of green.

Was the enemy out there? Were they watching? Waiting?

Our eyes darted up and down, side to side, capturing every shift of the bush, scrutinizing every rotted log. Our ears strained, analyzing every twig snap, every bird's call, every not-too-distant artillery blast.

Please don't let us be lost.

Ioli must have been thinking the same thing. "Where the hell are we?" he whispered.

"Quiet," Dirks shushed.

My heart was pounding so loud I thought I'd give us away.

Finally, we saw the outpost ahead. Stacks of sandbags, coils of wire. Slowly, carefully, we eased toward the guard gate.

Then the trees came alive. I could feel the adrenaline sear through my chest.

In an instant, we were surrounded by figures in camouflage, faces painted black, twigs atop their helmets, M16s locked and loaded.

Round eyes. Their sights on the jungle, not on our truck. Friendlies.

Breathe. In. Out. In. Out.

"Jesus, man," I said to one of them through the back flap, my heart still sprinting. I sounded like a child, my voice was so high, tight. "I didn't even see you guys out there!"

The soldier grinned, his teeth glowing unnaturally white against his shoe-polished face. "Soldier, we've been watching you for the last three miles."

He winked and disappeared back into the bush.

PLEIKU

We rolled into camp, still shaking. My shirt was so wet it felt like another skin.

"Baby Face, that you?"

Wash. He was at the front gate. I'd never been so glad to see a familiar face in my life. I wanted to climb out and hug him.

"Wash, how are you, man?" I said, trying to pull myself together. He walked around to my side of the truck and shook my hand—I don't think he noticed the trembling—through the window. He looked thin. And tired.

"I'm still here, so I must be doing okay," he said, flashing a grin. He stuck his head inside the window and looked around at all of us. "You guys all right? What's happening?"

"Just got an escort through the Pass," Dirks said. He held out his hand. "Dirks."

"Washington." They exchanged a soul-brother shake.

"Well, you look all in one piece, so I'm guessing the Road-runners brought you up." Dirks nodded. Then Wash tapped me playfully on the shoulder. "So what you all doing up here, Baby Face? How's Qui Nhon been treating you?"

"It's good," I said, my heart finally slowing to a trot. "Not too bad. We put together a band. A rock band."

"No way, that's you?" Wash grinned. "Captain told us we'd be getting some music this weekend. I'm telling you, the company's pumped. We don't get no entertainment, man. Just the fireworks and the air show, if you know what I mean. So, no kidding, they letting you play here?"

I nodded and tried to swallow.

"Well, you best let Needham know you're here. Captain's been waiting all day. Just move straight on through. Club's to the left. You'll find him."

"Thanks, man," I said. "We'll see you later."

"You know it," Wash said, and gave us a wave.

We drove into the compound, the others giving me grief about my old MP-school nickname, which Wash had just reminded them of. Anything to keep us from thinking about what we'd gotten ourselves into.

Then Dirks leaned out his window and gave a low whistle. "Would you take a look at that?"

Dug in the center of the compound was an underground bunker the size of an Olympic swimming pool, only twice as deep. Layers of sandbags covered the roof.

"Only one reason for something that fortified," Sugden said.

"Some serious action," Ioli answered.

I tried to push it out of my mind as we fell out of the truck.

Captain Needham was there to greet us. "You made it. Welcome to Pleiku, men." He waved his cigar. "I found a friend of yours."

Pridden was with him. His appearance was startling. He looked thirty pounds thinner and about thirty years older than when he left Dodge City. Like a skeleton in fatigues. He smiled wanly.

"Man, am I glad to see you guys," he said, reaching for an amp off the back of the truck. "Let me give you a hand."

"Take a good look at these soldiers."

Needham had us lined up in front of his troops, about a hundred guys, two platoons. Their grizzled faces and tired eyes followed him as he paced back and forth, gnawing on his stub of cigar.

"First rocket that comes over the compound, you get these five men down into the bunker. You throw your bodies over them. You make sure nothing happens to them. I promised their commander they wouldn't get hurt. And, goddammit, I keep my damned promises."

I glanced over at Ioli, Sugden, Jessen, Dirks. They looked just as uncomfortable as I was. Rockets? We were MPs, we knew how to take care of ourselves. Still, the captain thought we might be needing some help. What did that mean? That we could be in for some heavy action? Maybe performing here wasn't the smartest thing to do. Maybe we should do this some other time, when things weren't so . . . hot.

When Needham was done, I asked to speak with him away from his men. We walked toward the club where the rest of the band was starting to set up.

"Sir, are you sure it's a good idea that we play?" I asked. "I mean, we're pretty loud. And with the rockets and all. Won't it make it easier for the enemy to target the camp?"

Needham gave a slick grin and clapped a hand on my shoulder. "Soldier, Charlie screws with us nearly every night. Has been for months. We ain't no big surprise, he knows exactly where we are. And now we're gonna let him know that we don't give a rat's ass that he's out there. There's no intimidating the United States Army. Think of it as psyops, Kohler. We're gonna party, goddammit—and Charlie can go to hell. We're gonna rock Charlie's ass straight back to Hanoi. You got that?"

God, I don't want to die.

"Yes, sir," I said.

We were in the pocket, in the groove. Where one note led to the next and the next and the next and we could count on it always. Nobody shooting. Nobody dying. An armor of sound we pulled around us, tighter, closer—even as

228

explosions thundered outside the camp.

If I must die here, please, God, let me be making music when I go.

Sugden kicked out the familiar bassline and the GIs of Pleiku were hanging on the lyrics, leaning on our notes, riding our rhythms. We were all in it together. The chords swirling around us were a tornado. Tearing, pulling. Lifting us up and out, away from the rockets landing just beyond our perimeter. Out of the jungle, out of the country, out of this world. And we were at the center of it. All of us. Moving together, a force of our own, the music's pulse our collective heartbeat. Our togetherness trumping everything. Doubt. Fear. Death.

This was our anthem.

We were all on our feet, singing at the top of our lungs: *We gotta get out of this place. 'Cause, man, there's a better life for me and you.*

And when it was over, we fell together, Jon, Mike, Ben, and I. Exhausted, laughing. Laughing because we were all still alive.

The rocket fire finally faded as the sun came up. None had landed inside the camp. We played the next night without incident and made it safely back to Qui Nhon on Sunday—with the help of the Roadrunners—in just under three hours.

I'd never been so happy to see Dodge City.

WHO AM I?

"**M**en, as you know, I came to Fort Bragg last summer after having command of the 164th MP unit in Germany. I was fortunate enough to start this outfit with you, the 127th, and I will never forget this outfit."

We hadn't been back ten minutes before Captain had called the whole company to formation. Now he stood in front of us, pacing back and forth in the muggy afternoon heat.

"Men, you'll recall that back at Bragg we had no idea where in Vietnam we were going, so we trained in the field six days a week, from dark in the morning to dark at night. All of that hard work has paid off, soldiers. Look at you now. We started out with nothing, and you built Dodge City, you built this company, to what it is, what you are, today. Your commitment to your unit, your commitment to your country, your commitment to each other is something you can always be proud of, and it is something I will cherish until they throw the dirt on top of me."

Captain wasn't big on sentiment; tough-and-gruffness was kind of part of his job description. But there he was, waxing poetic about the 127th. We could tell something was up.

"I called all of you out here this afternoon because I have some news I need to share with you. It was my honor to learn this morning that I have been promoted to the rank of major. As often happens, the promotion came with a transfer. The army now needs my services over at Battalion Headquarters, so I am sorry to say that I will no longer have command of the 127th. As of"—he looked down at his watch—"twenty minutes ago, Lieutenant—make that Captain—Vedlitz is your new commanding officer."

It was startling news, totally unexpected. A ripple of stunned glances made its way across the ranks.

The 127th without Captain Leadbetter? It was hard to imagine.

Then Captain stood stock-still in front of us. He took off his sunglasses and looked out over the company.

"So, men, I can't thank you enough for the opportunity to serve with you. And I want you to know that I will remember our time here, our experience together, as long as I'm on the right side of the green grass." He bowed his head for a moment. Then he looked up, put his sunglasses on, and barked, "Dismissed!"

Sergeant Hall, standing up front near the captain, started to applaud. The whole company joined in.

And then Captain was gone.

We hadn't even gotten a chance to tell him about Pleiku.

"So how's it going with Lynda?" Leach asked from behind the wheel. "You still seeing her?" We were headed back to Dodge City after working the midnight to 0800 prisoner patrol at the EVAC hospital.

I was glad the night had been quiet. Ever since Pleiku, the band guys and I had been really jumpy. We didn't really talk about it. We just wanted to forget it.

Now the sun was up and we were tired.

"Yeah, I'm still seeing her, but it's getting weird," I told Leach, rubbing my eyes to stay awake.

"Like how?"

I thought about it for a second. "Well, for one thing, she's asking all sorts of questions about the States, about Virginia. About my town and my neighborhood and my family."

He adjusted the rearview mirror. "That's weird?"

"Well, yeah. It's like she's making plans. Like she's going to be there someday. With me."

Leach was quiet. I looked out over the paddies rolling by.

"She's getting too close, you know what I mean? She's

acting like we're going steady or something. If I don't stop in for a few days, she pouts, like I need to make things up to her. You know, like a girlfriend."

Leach didn't say anything.

"I thought we were just having fun, you know?"

Leach nodded.

"And she's got a strange look in her eyes these days. I don't know what it is, exactly."

He turned onto the road into camp. "Love?"

"Maybe. More like . . . desperation."

We were both quiet.

I had the feeling that I wasn't Lynda's first soldier, not the first GI she'd seen as her ticket out. That maybe some other guy had toyed with her. Made her promises. Left her.

Time to back away.

The next day I was in the barracks flipping through *Hit Parader*.

The Monkees were recording a new album. Six hundred million fans saw the Beatles sing "Love Is All You Need" on TV. Peter Noone of Herman's Hermits was filming a movie. Dave Davies of the Kinks was cutting a solo record.

It all seemed so far away. Like something out of a fairy tale. Didn't anyone know we were over here? That there was a war going on? That people were dying?

Artillery echoed off the mountains. We were hearing it more often these days, the rhythmic pounding, the hollow boom of explosions. Sometimes we'd look up and see a jet streaking past the mountain, then hear the blasts, like cymbals crashing, far off but still too near.

I put down the magazine and listened. The sound rumbled through me, into me, making me feel small and alone. The lump in my gut, the hard ball that never went away now, pushed at my insides. I took a deep breath, trying to quell the queasiness.

I turned to the classifieds. A tiny ad down in the corner caught my eye.

CONVERT YOUR TAPES TO 45 RPM DISCS
2 SIDES FOR $3.00
MINIMUM ORDER 10

It was someplace in Indiana. If you sent them your tape, they'd make you a 45 rpm record. The ad was so small, I almost missed it, buried between the six-dollar dress shirts and the X-ray Specs.

But all of a sudden it was the most important thing in the world.

A record. In Vietnam.

I closed my eyes and bowed my head. Goodridge floated into my mind.

You're a musician, not a killer.

Am I?

I'm a soldier.

And what the hell did that mean? I'd been in Vietnam for ten months now, with hardly any action compared to other guys. Still, I'd seen things—terrifying things—I could never have imagined seeing. Done things I could never have fathomed doing. Thought things I could never have contemplated before.

I wasn't the same person who came to Vietnam back in January.

Now I was somebody else. Somebody I wasn't sure I wanted to be.

Dad, are you proud of me?

Mom, would you know me?

Roy, what would you think of me?

The recording contract and the Satellites seemed as if they were all from another lifetime, another reality. Maybe it was something I imagined a long time ago. Maybe it was one of those dreams that starts out warm and happy, makes you smile in your sleep, but then somewhere in the middle gets all mixed up and turned around until you wake up cold and trembling and reaching for the light switch.

A thunder roll of shelling rang beyond the mountain.

Will my dream end here in Vietnam?

Will my life end here in Vietnam?

We had to make a record.

"So, what do you think?" I said, bracing for the wrong answer.

Ioli tossed the magazine back to me from behind the drums. He grinned from ear to ear. "A forty-five! What are you kidding? Hell, yeah!"

Ioli—I could always count on him.

"So we'd need to order enough to make it work," I said, grabbing my guitar. "I figure I'd buy two."

"I'll buy a couple." Jessen powered up the Farfisa.

"I'm in," Sugden said, pulling his new bass from the case. It was an imitation Höfner, like the one Paul McCartney played. He'd picked it up at Papasan's. "I'll take two."

"You can put me down for a deuce, bay-*beee*!" Ioli twirled a stick over his head.

"Okay, so that's eight," I said. "Two more, and we can do this thing."

Leach snapped a reel onto the tape deck. "I'm in for one."

"Nine," I said.

Everybody turned to McClory, leaning back in a folding chair in the corner.

He threw his hands up. "Okay. I'll take one."

A series of rumbles rattled the supply tent.

"Damn, sounds close," Sugden muttered, his voice tense.

We glanced out the screening toward the mountain. We didn't see anything. We looked the other way, down into camp. Everything was the same. Guys were sauntering off toward the motor pool, others were heading in and out of the mess hall, a few rebounded baskets from the hoop Captain had appropriated for us before he left. The shelling continued—and life went on at Dodge City.

Jessen looked jittery. He rolled a few arpeggios across the keyboard, his eyes darting to the hills. "So . . . what do you guys want to record? What should we put on a Banana record?"

"A Banana record," Ioli said with a sort of laugh. "Who ever thought we'd be making a record?"

"Whoever thought we'd be playing in a band?" Jessen said. "Not me."

I pulled the guitar strap over my shoulder. "I don't want to cover any radio hits, no Top Forty. It's got to be something special. Nothing cheesy."

"Right," Sugden said. He thumbed a string with one hand and twisted a tuning peg with the other. "This needs to be totally Banana."

Ioli turned to me. "How about one of your songs?"

I thought about it for a second and shrugged.

"Yeah, how about 'She's Gone'?" Jessen suggested.

An old one. I'd written it for the Satellites. It was going to be one of the sides of the Tower single.

"Are you sure?" I said. "This is supposed to be a Banana record, not a Dean Kohler record."

"The Banana does 'She's Gone,'" Jessen said.

"Yeah, it's one of our best songs," Ioli added.

I turned to Sugden. "What do you think?"

"Works for me," he said, lighting up a cigarette and glancing outside again.

"All right," I said. "What else?"

Everyone was quiet.

"What about the Velvets?" Leach suggested.

"Yeah, 'There She Goes Again' is cool." Jessen moved through the chords of the chorus.

Ioli added a beat. "Yeah, man, Velvet Underground."

Shells boomed like kettledrums.

"Jeez," Sugden grumbled, "let's do this before Charlie comes to dinner."

We ran through the songs a couple of times. And then we were ready.

Ready to make a record.

Leach checked the tape and hit the red RECORD button. "Rolling," he said.

I swallowed hard.

I launched the song, Jessen's organ chord ringing warm and gentle under my guitar. Sugden slipped in on bass, filling in the spaces, then Ioli brought in the snare and the gently tripping hi-hat cymbal.

The booming outside answered us, but we didn't care.

We were making a record.

It hit me all at once—the reality of what we were doing—as I sang . . .

I don't know the reason why she's gone
Guess she realized she couldn't go on
I guess she didn't know I still love her so
She's gone
Everything I do turns out wrong
I guess she realized we couldn't go on
I didn't realize as I looked in her eyes
She's gone
If you see her tell her just for me
Tell her I still want her
Just the way she used to be
Tell her I still care
She's gone
She's gone
She's gone

When the song was over, Leach stopped the tape. We looked at one another.

No one said a word.

We didn't have to. Our eyes said it all.

THE RECORD

It was 0100, late, and Ioli and I were returning from the 1600-to-midnight shift at the hospital out in the Valley. Cong prisoner patrol had been uneventful and we were headed back to Dodge City, ready to hit the rack.

I swung out onto the shortcut. Force of habit—I always went that way—a right turn onto a winding dirt road that hugged the base of the mountain. To our left was the lake and the jungle beyond that. It was a beautiful setting, especially so on this night, the water smooth and glassy, a thin sliver of a moon glittering across the surface. It occurred to me that it was the first time I'd ever driven the shortcut at night.

We couldn't see anything beyond the headlights. Everything to our rear was pitch-black. My skin started to prickle. I was getting a bad feeling. Who was out there, watching?

"Maybe taking the shortcut at night wasn't the best idea,"

I whispered to Ioli, the cold stone pressing on my gut.

"Yeah," he whispered back, "let's get out of here."

I opened up the jeep.

And bullets flew.

"Holy—!" Ioli yelped, and dove down in his seat.

We were taking gunfire from across the lake. Rounds cracked all around us, slapping at the earth, ricocheting with metallic *zings* off the jeep. The blasts echoed across the Valley. A shot ripped past my ear, so close I could feel the heat.

I tried not to whimper.

God, no, not again. I can't do this anymore. I can't . . .

I'd sunk low in the seat, breathless, still driving, keeping us moving.

The bullets kept coming.

God, I'm not ready to die.

I felt Ioli's hand on my knee. He was holding on to it like a lifeline.

I forced my mind to go blank, and I let the training take over.

I switched off the headlights. The road disappeared. It was so dark I thought my eyes were closed, even though they were wide open. I knew there was a good chance I was either going to run into the mountain or drive out into the lake.

"I can't see a damn thing!" I gasped. I cut the engine and hit the jeep floor next to Ioli. I could feel him shaking, like I was.

A few more shots rang out. Then, quiet.

I put my hand on Ioli's shoulder. "Take cover behind the jeep," I hissed.

I felt him reach for his rifle. I groped around for mine.

Silently, we slid out of the vehicle, M14s in hand. We held our fire, not wanting to give away our position.

"Congs don't give up that easily," I whispered. "Something's up."

"You think they're coming this way?"

My gut clenched.

"I don't know. Too dark to tell."

We stared out into the blackness, searching for any sign, any movement. Our ears strained for any telltale sound. All we heard was insect drone.

"We've got to get out of here."

Ioli was glued to his rifle sight. I reached into the console and grabbed a pop flare. If we illuminated the area on their side of the lake, we'd have enough light to slip away without headlights and without giving ourselves away. If we saw somebody move, we could get a couple of shots off.

"I'll do it." Ioli took the flare from me.

He removed the top, slid the top onto the bottom, pulled it back a couple of inches, then smacked the bottom with his other hand.

The flare flew across the lake, landing on a large tree on the far side of the water. The tree burst into flames.

In the black smoke and fiery orange glow, we could just

make out two figures sprinting out of the brush under the tree.

We both emptied our full magazines in about five seconds. As the tree blazed, the two shadows disappeared into the jungle.

"Mike, man," I gasped, "I don't remember anything in MP school about setting trees on fire to deal with snipers."

Ioli gave me a weary grin and slapped me on the top of the head.

"Shut up and get in the jeep."

Two weeks seemed like two years, but finally the records arrived.

I carried the box back to the barracks like it was a wedding cake.

Sugden saw the box in my hand and raised his eyebrows.

I nodded.

I placed the box on my bunk. We stared at it for a few moments.

"You gonna open it?" Sugden said softly.

I breathed deep. "Yeah."

The low thunder of distant artillery rumbled off the mountain.

I ripped off the tape. Pulled apart the flaps.

I lifted out the discs, carefully, my fingers on the edges. Black vinyl gleamed, a faint iridescent rainbow glittering through the shiny grooves.

A record. *Our* record.

I handed one to Sugden.

He cracked a wide grin. "Let's get over to Suttle's."

A group of guys gathered around Suttle's footlocker. Leach, McClory, Giant, Voina, Sanchez, a few others. Suttle dropped the phonograph needle.

I held my breath.

The sound rang crisp and clear from the tiny stereo speakers.

"She's Gone." It was all there. All perfect. My jingle-jangle Byrds guitar. The melancholy "Ticket to Ride" swirl. The sweet backing vocals.

And, on the flip, "There She Goes Again." The Lou-Reed-cool sing-speak. The spiny rhythms. The swinging time-signature change-out to the end.

When the needle lifted, everybody clapped and hooted and cheered. They slapped us on the back, punched us playfully on the arms.

"Play it again!" Leach shouted.

I felt strange. Like I was melting. Like something was dissolving in my chest.

Be cool.

I blinked, then blinked again as my song started back up.

Don't cry, don't cry.

Sugden thumped me on the shoulder. "Sounds pretty damn good."

"Yeah," I said, turning away, certain the others could see everything I didn't want them to.

I was back at our barracks. Sugden had left for duty. Nobody else was around.

I couldn't stop looking at the records. I pulled them out and held them. I flipped them over and over in my hands, feeling their slight weight, admiring their licorice sheen.

Something wasn't quite right, though. Something was missing.

Labels.

I dug out the lettering kit I used to make First Sergeant's charts, plus a pencil and a compass. I wandered the empty barracks, prowling. I gathered a stack of magazines, grabbing what was lying around, under bunks, on top of footlockers, scattered across the table in the common area.

I took a seat at the table and flipped through each one, page by page, searching for just what I needed: color pages with lots of image area and no words. *Hit Parader, Song Hits, Car and Driver*, no. *Popular Mechanics, Field and Stream*, no.

Playboy. Yes. Full-page spreads with lots of clean, colored areas.

I traced ten perfect circles, then cut them out with scissors from my survival sewing kit. I hand-lettered THE BANANA and the song titles on each label. Then I glued them on the records. When I was finished, every disc looked different, each a small, round work of art.

I picked up the brightest one, the one with the red and orange and yellow label. I slipped it back into its white paper sleeve. Pressed it between two pieces of cardboard torn from the box.

I slid it into a large USO mailing envelope and addressed it to Roy Ellis.

FAREWELLS

My dear,

    I love you.

    I wish for the day to end quickly so I can be near you and then I want the time to go slowly to make the joys of being near you last longer.

    Come to see me soon.

    Love,

    Lynda

Giant brought me the letter. He'd stopped in at the Lyndabar. Lynda had given it to him to give to me.

I read it again.

I folded it up and locked it away in my cabinet, behind the Rice Krispies from Mom.

* * *

It was my turn to pick up the band money from Steinmetz at MACV.

"Ioli tells me you men are leaving in December," he said, handing me a receipt to sign. "That's just a few weeks."

"Yes, sir."

"Well, I gotta tell you, you'll be missed. Other than a couple of acts I've brought over from the States, you guys have been the only entertainment most of those soldiers have had all year."

"Thank you, sir. We've enjoyed playing for them, sir."

Steinmetz leaned back in his desk chair and put his arms behind his head. Then he made the Banana an offer. If we'd transfer over to Special Services, he said, he'd promote all of us to E-5 and send us on a year-long concert tour of army bases around the world.

Before I could even think about it, I found myself turning him down. If he would've asked me a year and a half ago, I'd have said yes in a second. But now, even though I'd never asked to be a soldier, I knew that's what I was. As much as I wanted out, I needed to finish my duty.

Fourteen days and a wake-up.

If I could make it two more weeks, I'd be back to "the world."

Release the PAUSE *button. Put life back on* PLAY.

It was a day off for me and I had big plans. I'd hit the beach one last time and then maybe shop downtown for souvenirs to take back home.

Home. I almost didn't want to think about it, I didn't want to jinx it. But it was always on my mind now. I wondered what it would be like, if it would be just as I'd remembered it. Would I fit back in, like a puzzle piece that'd been lost under the sofa for months? I headed out the barracks door. If I hurried, I could catch a shuttle jeep to the beach over at the motor pool.

I ran smack-dab into Lupica—with Lynda.

"Dean!" she cried.

She loves me.

I don't love her.

I hadn't been to Lyndabar in weeks. Now I didn't know what to say.

"What are you doing here?" It was all I could think of.

"Your friend"—she gave Lupica's arm a tug—"he brought me here. I've been wanting to see you."

Great. I was trying to disappear with as little mess as possible, and Lupica was dragging Lynda to the base.

I glared at Lupica. He gave me a smirk. I felt the slow burn start up in my stomach.

Lynda touched my chest. She searched my face, her lids brimming.

"I miss you," she said softly. Her lips trembled. I could see the hurt in her eyes.

I never wanted to hurt anybody.

"Where have you been?" she asked.

Damn, this is uncomfortable. Think, think, think.

"Well," I stalled, "I've been working a lot."

She looked down. "Oh."

Man, I'm no good at these good-bye things. Why can't she just take the hint?

"Oh, yeah," Lupica jumped in, nasal whine oozing sarcasm. "You know how they work the short-timers. Never a moment's rest. Don't want 'em to get too lazy before they ship 'em back home. Ha!"

Lynda looked up. "Home? You mean America? Dean, you are going home soon?"

Swell. Now the cat was out of the bag. So much for a quick, painless end to the thing.

Thanks a freakin' lot, Lupica.

"Um, yeah," I soft-shoed.

I need to get out of here. Now.

"I still have some time left, though." I glanced at my watch. "Look, I've got to get going. They're waiting on me over at the motor pool."

Suddenly Lynda wrapped her arms around my neck. Her tears spilled and she kissed me deeply.

"You come see me again," she whispered in my ear.

"Um, yeah. Okay," I said. "See you around."

I turned on my heel and didn't look back.

THE LAST GIG

We chose the army signal company out at the edge of town for our last gig because it was our favorite place to play. The stage at the enlisted club was large, there were dressing rooms, and the guys there loved us. Vedlitz—thrilled, we were sure, that the band was soon to be history—gave permission for Leach and McClory to come with us. Leach brought his tape recorder, and McClory agreed to shoot footage with the eight-millimeter movie camera I'd bought at the PX. We wanted to make our last gig a real show, so we brought three costume changes—our regular street clothes for the first set, the shirts from Sugden's wife for the second, and the Banana outfits for the finale.

We set up our equipment, ran through a sound check, then huddled at the end of the bar as the place started to fill. A lot of the faces were familiar: soldiers who'd come to all of our shows. But there were a lot of new guys too.

"You gonna say anything?" Ioli asked me, tipping his beer can toward the crowd. "Let 'em know this is the end, you know?"

I looked around at the soldiers pouring into the club. They were talking among themselves, buzzing, excited, looking forward to a night of release, of relief. Why should we spoil their experience?

I shook my head. "No, man. We don't need to bring anyone down. Best to ride out the Banana on a high note." I smiled. "No pun intended. Give 'em a show they'll never forget."

Ioli lifted his beer. "I second that, baby!"

The bartender handed Sugden another brew. Sug toasted Ioli. "To the Electrical Banana." Jessen raised his beer. I lifted my Coke.

"Peeled and about to split," Jessen said with a grin. We all groaned.

"The shocking end!" Ioli added, and we groaned again. We tapped our cans together.

And then we hit the stage.

The crowd was with us from the first note. Guys were singing along, clapping, waving their beers in the air. Rowdy cheers and whistles erupted at the end of every tune. By the fifth song, the whole club seemed to be vibrating to the beat.

And this is the last time.

Something stuck in my throat. I swallowed hard as I

252

came back in on vocals.

At the end of our last set, the crowd wouldn't let us leave. We did three encores, then everyone wanted to talk and hang out. The bar manager finally had to shoo everyone from the club.

"We did it, man," Ioli said as the last soldier staggered out the door. "We rocked 'em."

We took our time packing up. We didn't say much.

Jessen was the first to go.

The Farfisa had been shipped back to the Jessen family home in New Jersey. We sold the amps and drums to a couple of Air Force guys who wanted the gear for their base recreation department.

Ben was packing the last of his things into his duffel.

The rest of us were silent. What could we say? We had made it through the fear and the blood and the explosions and the gunfire. Through the music and the performances and the cheering and applause. We had made soldiers smile and watched soldiers die. We had made it through together, all of us, the best that we could. And we'd made it out to the other side.

"Maybe we can get together sometime," Ioli offered, "back in 'the world.' After Ben and I get out. Play some music." He tapped out a drumroll on his mattress. "You know, rock and roll again."

Sugden cleaned his glasses with his T-shirt. "Yeah. Sure."

"Sounds good," I said, tossing Jessen some paperbacks I'd borrowed months ago. He shoved them into his pack.

Deep down, though, we all knew it would never happen. Because they had enlisted, Uncle Sam had Ioli and Jessen for another whole year. And even after they got out, we all lived hundreds of miles from one another. We had been strangers when we'd met. Now, in a way, we felt like strangers again.

Jessen closed the duffel. He took a last long look around the barracks.

We all stood up. One by one we embraced him and wished him luck, told him to keep in touch, to let us know where the army sent him next.

"Well," he finally said, "I guess this is it."

And then it was done.

I felt lost.

The Banana was really over.

December 15, 1967.

I boarded a C-130 at the airbase in Qui Nhon, along with Sanino from supply and McDaniels. It was a quick hop over to Cam Ranh Bay, where we'd catch a commercial airliner for the flight home.

Home. It still hadn't sunk in yet.

They fed us lunch at Cam Ranh Bay. We walked into the mess hall, decorated with streamers and colored Christmas lights, and the first thing we noticed was half gallons of fresh milk in the center of each table. Real milk. We hadn't seen it in a year. I picked up a carton to see where it was packaged. Hawaii. The States.

Roast beef, mashed potatoes, peas, chocolate cake with ice cream. Paperwork. Sign here. Sign there.

And then boarding time.

I looked out the window. The mountains loomed gray in the distance, their dark secrets hidden behind a veil of silver mist. Missing limbs, pools of blood, gaping holes. Secrets that I locked away in my head, that I folded and buried deep in my heart.

The engines revved and the plane taxied down the steel runway.

A cheer went up as we broke through the mist. I couldn't speak. The mountains receded until they were mere bumps on a carpet of green and gray.

We refueled at an Air Force base in Japan, then it was a straight shot to Seattle. Early on December 16, we landed at Fort Lewis, Washington.

The United States of America.

I closed my eyes and inhaled. Held the breath deep inside of me. Let it out.

We stood in line at the processing center, where most soldiers were being reassigned to their next duty station. I was one of the lucky ones. I had less than ninety days remaining of my obligation to Uncle Sam—I was at eighty-nine—so I was to be processed out, the remaining active-duty days dropped.

Thank God for small favors.

I looked for a phone booth to call home, to let my parents know that I was safely on the ground in the United States. Long lines streamed from the crowded banks of pay phones. I waited. And waited. It was 2100 hours, nearly midnight in Virginia, when it was finally my turn.

Mom answered.

It was the first time I'd heard her voice in a year.

"Dean, is that you?"

She sounded the same, as if the clock had been reset and we were back at the kitchen table having breakfast.

It felt strange, foreign.

"Mom, I'm in Seattle . . ."

I could tell she was trying to keep from crying on the other end of the line. I told her I was okay, that I'd be home soon.

"Your father wants to talk to you," she said, and handed the phone over.

"Dean?"

I pressed my lips together and closed my eyes, fighting back tears. I took a deep breath.

"Hi, Dad."

I was almost home, yet I felt like I was still on the other side of the world. I wanted to reach out, to touch him, to feel him hug me. To hear him tell me he was proud of me.

Instead, we talked about the transportation from Vietnam to Seattle. Small talk.

He put Mary on. Everyone's fine, she told me. Everyone can't wait to see me.

And what will they see?

Boy? Man? Soldier? Musician? Killer?

I hung up and got back in line at the ticket desk.

"I'm sorry, there are still no military standby seats available," the lady told me again. "There are a few first-class seats available, leaving in an hour . . ."

I pulled out my wallet and fingered the bills. I had three months of processing-out pay plus a travel allowance on me, all in cash.

"First class will be fine," I said.

COMING HOME

I woke up as we were taxiing to the terminal. I looked out the window. The sky was pink behind black stripes of trees with no leaves. A flock of birds lifted from the skeleton branches. Through the trees, I could see water, glistening like a rice paddy. Except it wasn't a paddy, it was the lagoon at the Norfolk Botanical Garden, where Judy and I'd rented a rowboat once and spent a lazy summer afternoon making out among the lily pads and lotus blossoms.

I was home.

The pilot's voice crackled over the intercom. "Welcome to Norfolk International Airport. . . ."

Virginia looked the same. I was totally different.

I straightened my uniform and adjusted the wedge-shaped garrison cap on my head.

It was cold. The wind whipped at my face as I descended the rollaway steps. I pulled my army trench coat tighter around me. My eyes scanned the terminal building across the gray tarmac.

And I saw them, haloed in the airport floodlights.

Mom and Mary, waving.

Dad.

Smiling.

Proud.

All of a sudden, nothing mattered.

I'd made it back. I'd done what I had to do. I'd done it on my own. And now I was home.

Mom ran up to hug me. She held me for a long time, so choked up she could barely speak. Mary was next. Then Dad.

He held me close.

"Welcome home, son," he said, his voice cracking. "Welcome home."

I didn't speak. I was afraid if I said one thing, I'd end up crying in his arms like a little kid. Which was exactly what I felt like.

So I hugged him back.

Way back on March 14, 1966, the day I left for boot camp, I'd already written off the next two years of my life—a year of training, a year in Nam. Family. Friends. Music. All of it.

Now my life could resume.

First on the agenda: a new car.

Dad loaned me his Catalina. I headed to McLean Pontiac in Portsmouth. Smokey's dad didn't work there anymore, they told me. They didn't have anything I liked. The salesmen weren't even interested in talking to me. Where would a kid like me get the money to afford a GTO? I headed over to Roughton Pontiac in Norfolk.

There it was. In the showroom, surrounded by five other new Pontiacs. My GTO. Gold, beautiful.

I peered inside, admiring the leather interior. I ran my hand over the fastback, ogled the dual hood scoops and the headlights hidden in the split grille.

The salesman handed me the keys. "Take a ride."

"Me?" The car was so gorgeous, I was almost afraid to drive it. Almost.

I cruised down three blocks, stopped on a side street, then smoked the tires all the way down the block.

Yeah. This baby's mine.

The sales guy was standing outside when I pulled back into the dealership. I eased up to the curb.

He leaned in my open window. "Back already? Go on, take it for a ride!"

Roger that.

I headed for the tunnel to Portsmouth. Within minutes I was pulling up in our driveway.

Dad came out.

I was expecting him to hate the car. To tell me that it wasn't practical. That it was too flashy. Overpriced.

"She's pretty," he said, surprising me. "Is this the one?"

I'd never bought a car before. I'd dropped a few hundred on a guitar. But the GTO was stickered at $4,345. And I knew the salesman was going to try to work me over. I was twenty, but I still looked like I was about sixteen.

Even after a year in Nam, I felt I needed the guidance of my dad.

"Come with me to the dealership?" I asked him.

We drove back over to Norfolk. Dad talked the sales guy down and closed the deal. I wrote a check for the total—nearly two years of army pay and Banana money. We drove back to Portsmouth, me in my new GTO, Dad following in his Catalina.

Dad insisted I park the GTO in the garage.

He took the driveway.

When we got inside, I called Judy to ask her for a date, my first date in two years.

"Hi, it's Dean."

There was a pause. As if she was trying to place the name, the voice.

Then Judy said, "Oh! Oh my gosh, you're back. How are you?"

Her voice sounded different. Not like I remembered. Older, like a teacher or something.

"I'm good," I said, wondering if I sounded different too. "How have you been? How are things?"

"I'm fine," she said. Another pause, like she was thinking of something to say. "When did you get back?"

"Day before yesterday," I said.

"That's nice," she said. "Just in time for Christmas." The way she said it, it sounded like she was chatting with someone in line at the post office or something.

I wished I could see her face. I thought maybe I should have gone over to her house instead of calling her up.

Forget me not.

Lynda flashed in my mind, then vanished. I knew I had no right to think it, that it didn't really matter, but I wondered if Judy had been with anyone else.

"I got a car," I blurted out.

"Oh, that's nice," she said. "A new car."

"Yeah, it's a GTO." I paused. "Gold. With gold leather interior."

"That's nice." She sounded far away.

"Yeah. I thought maybe you might want to go for a ride. Go up to Rexall's for a soda or something."

"Now?" She sounded alarmed.

"Yeah," I said. "If you're not doing anything. If you want to. It would be good to see you," I added.

She was quiet for a few seconds. "Um, yeah. I guess that would be all right."

"Okay," I said. I guess I had expected something more.

Judy didn't say anything.

"Pick you up in, say, half an hour?"

Another pause. "Sure," she said. "See you then."

She hung up the phone.

Judy took another sip of her Coke and looked down at the metal counter, doodling on the paper place mat with the handle of her spoon. "Happy Together," the Turtles, came on the jukebox.

Judy looked great, prettier than I remembered. She was wearing her hair a little longer, with the ends kind of flipped up. Her pink sweater showed off her curves. Even though she sat across the booth from me, I could smell her—warm, clean, like soap.

When she'd answered the door at her house, she'd given me a stiff hug.

Out in the driveway, Judy had complimented me on the car. Then at Rexall's she'd caught me up on old friends and all the things that had happened while I was away, like who'd gotten married and who'd gone off to college and that Joey Wentz had to repeat his senior year because he'd flunked out of both English and algebra, even though he'd aced shop. She didn't say anything about who'd gone off to the war or who hadn't come back.

She'd gone on about graduation and how she'd won the Miss Cradock contest at school. She'd asked about my parents, about Mary, about Roy.

And now there didn't seem to be anything left to talk about.

I knew she didn't want to hear about the war. About what I had done, what I had seen. Not that I would have told her. But she didn't even ask.

I folded my napkin into fourths, then eighths, and then sixteenths. Before the war it had been so easy to talk to Judy; our conversations had come so naturally.

But now Judy and me, it seemed like it was just a memory. I'd spent the last year seeing what most people shouldn't; she'd spent them at parties and football games and drive-ins.

I felt remote, distant, like I was sitting on an island in the middle of the sea. Like we had absolutely nothing in common anymore.

"Thanks for the letter you sent," I said.

"Oh. You're welcome." She took another sip. "Thanks for writing back."

I nodded and fell silent.

She looked up and smiled. "Did I tell you we're moving to Maine?"

I shook my head. "Really?"

She nodded and her eyes lit up. "Mom got a job up there. It's real close to my grandparents and my aunt and cousins." She seemed excited. She was talking fast. "Mom says the town is really great. It's on the coast and there's a community college. Ginny, one of my cousins, goes there. She says it's really cool. I'm already signed up for some classes after winter break. Then maybe I might go on to the University of Maine, if I can get a scholarship or something." Her voice trailed off and she looked out the window at the parking lot.

I guess I was sad that she was leaving. But mostly, I felt relieved.

"Sounds great," I said.

I drove Judy home.

She gave me a quick kiss on the cheek and closed the door behind her.

Billy Ivey, an old high-school buddy, stopped by the next day. He was just back from Nam too. We were sitting in Mom's living room when a furniture truck went rumbling down the street. Right in front of our house, the truck backfired. Billy hit the floor, all 220 pounds of him, scrambling for the three-inch clearance under the green sofa.

He stood up, looking sheepish. "Sorry," he said. "I guess I'm not used to being home yet."

I told him about how when Mom asked me to help her in the yard that morning, I'd checked the flower beds for booby traps.

ADRIFT

"**D**o you want a sandwich? Can I cook you something?"

Mom was really glad to have me at home, waiting on me hand and foot, but it had been three weeks. Christmas was gone. New Year's was over. And now I could feel Dad watching me. Waiting to see what I'd do.

The thing was, I didn't know what to do.

"That's my boy, chip off the ol' block, private to specialist in less than a year," Dad would boast to all of my aunts and uncles, his friends down at the waterworks office, neighbors, the milkman, anybody who would listen to him. "Did I tell you about his Good Conduct medal? Came in the mail the other day."

But Dad hadn't said a single word about the Banana. Not that I thought he would. Any time he heard me talking about the band, like when Roy wanted to hear the full story behind the Banana record, Dad just disappeared behind his newspaper or turned on the TV news.

I knew he would be ecstatic if I went back into the service. Back into the army or his navy.

I didn't mind being an MP. I'd been surprised to find that I was pretty good at it. I'd proved something, to myself, to Dad. That I could do what my country asked of me. That I could do what a man had to do. But the military as a career? No way.

The shipyard? Compared to what I'd just done for the last two years, it seemed as boring as working on an assembly line.

College? Uncle Sam would pay for it. But there was no way I could sit in a classroom. Not now.

There was only one thing I really knew how to do. That I really wanted to do.

Music.

Same as it had ever been. Same as I knew it always would be.

I was spending most of my time jamming with some old musician buddies. I was sure Dad wasn't too happy about it. The Satellites were definitely history. Cecil had three months left in the army. Nobody knew where Cliff was. And Lynde had gone away to college. So I'd found some other guys to play with.

It was good to be playing again. But we were miles away from the Satellites.

Or the Banana.

* * *

Toward the end of January I got a letter from Jessen.

> Hi Dean,
>   Both Mike and I are out. I don't see too much of him, he's quite henpecked over some girl at Monmouth. I got engaged to my used-to-be best buddy's girl, don't worry, nobody can hook me for too long, but I dig her.
>   Take care,
>   Ben

He sounded good. Excited for the future. A guy with plans.

Meanwhile, I felt like a shipwreck survivor. Alive but adrift. Nowhere to go, no one to see.

I was happy for him.

Tet. It was all over the news. The NVA and VC made a massive surprise attack, more than a hundred towns and cities, all at the same time. They'd timed it to coincide with Tet, the big New Year holiday in Vietnam on January 31, so that all the ARVN guys would be on leave. We were beating them back, but it was looking messy. Really messy. Hundreds of GIs were dead; thousands of South Vietnamese were caught in the crossfire. I thought of Lynda and wondered if she was okay.

Qui Nhon was hit. It was in the newspaper. The ammo-supply depot out in the Valley got it first. Then the city itself was attacked, the enemy taking over the radio and railroad stations. The 93rd MP Battalion installation got nailed with mortars on February 1. There was fighting in the streets for days, the paper said.

And then an item about the 127th.

> On February 3, Lt. Dingus Banks Jr. of the 127th Military Police Company was fatally wounded by AK-47 gunfire to the chest as he attempted to flush a sniper from a building in downtown Qui Nhon. Banks was participating in combined police patrol activities with the Vietnamese National Police . . . fierce fighting . . . bodies in the streets . . . Americans and South Vietnamese . . .

I was stunned. I couldn't take my eyes off the pictures. Buildings I used to pass by every day were blown out. Heaps of rubble. M42 "duster" tanks rolling through streets I used to patrol.

I read and reread and read again. I didn't know Dingus. He had probably been one of our replacements.

It was sinking in. If not for my early out, that could have been me.

I was so glad to be out of there. So glad to be alive. So . . . grateful.

I put down the paper.

It was time to get on with my life.

MAKING PEACE

The next morning I parked my GTO outside the Portsmouth Employment Commission, the Who's "I Can
See for Miles" on the radio.

I walked inside.

"May I help you?" asked a gray-haired lady in red lipstick. She had a cigarette in her mouth.

"I'm looking for a job."

She peered at me over cat's-eye glasses on a chain.

"And what kind of work do you do?"

*Well, let's see, for the last two years I've avoided enemy
fire, swept for VC snipers, kept GIs safe, and toured with a
rock band through the jungles of Vietnam.*

I wasn't exactly sure what kind of work I did.

She shuffled papers on her desk, opened and closed
drawers. She dug through her purse, extracted a rhinestone-
studded lighter, and lit her smoke. On a small black-and-

white television behind her desk, the volume turned low, Desi Arnaz told Lucille Ball that he was home.

TV. Why not? "Are there any positions available at a television station?" I asked.

The lady exhaled a stream of smoke and cackled.

"Oh, no, dear. The TV stations never call us. They never have any problem finding people."

I must have looked disappointed, or she must have been feeling helpful that day. She said, "Why don't you just go on over to WAVY TV and ask? You know, Channel Ten? They're only a couple of blocks away, on Middle Street."

A few minutes later, I walked through the TV station's front door.

My job was to operate the RCA videotape machines and 16 mm projectors whenever we were taping or playing back shows or commercials. My shift hours weren't as great as promised. I worked a couple of weekdays, a couple of nights, plus weekends. But it wasn't bad. And it was a real job. Dad couldn't have been happier.

The weekend part really put a damper on dating. Judy was gone. I'd been hanging out a lot with Margaret, a pretty blonde. We'd been in the same art class in high school. Her family seemed pleased that we were dating. When she introduced me to her grandfather, a World War II veteran, and mentioned that I'd just returned from Vietnam, he got all teary-eyed, shaking my hand and saying, "We really appreciate what you guys are doing over there."

I saw both sides, though. A lot of people weren't happy about the war, staging protests about the thousands of American soldiers who'd gotten killed over there, saying that we shouldn't be involved in another country's civil war. If I happened to be in a store or a burger joint or somewhere and overheard the war being discussed, I just stayed out of it. I looked so young that even if someone glanced over and noticed me, they'd have no idea I'd already been over there. That I'd seen the war, lived the war. That it was still inside of me, wrapped up and stored away. I didn't want to talk about it anymore. I didn't want to think about it anymore. I just wanted to move on.

Not long after I'd started my WAVY job, I was working the late shift one Saturday night. We'd just finished the news at 2300 hours. But something was going on. Instead of turning off the studio lights like we usually did, the crew was setting up props and lighting a different area of the studio.

I hit my paging switch.

"Maury, what's up?" I said into my headset. "What are we doing?"

WAVY's top director paged me back from the control room.

"Gene Loving has a concert tonight down at the Virginia Beach Dome. He's bringing the group here afterward to tape an insert for *Disc-O-Ten*. It won't take long."

Gene Loving was the afternoon-drive disc jockey at WGH, one of the big radio stations in town. He was also a concert promoter—like the show at the Dome tonight—and cohost of WAVY's weekly dance program, *Disc-O-Ten*.

This could be cool.

When we were done setting up, I headed back to engineering. Two guys in black velvet suits were standing by my desk. One was checking out all the equipment, the oscilloscopes, the control panels. The other was staring at the video monitors.

"Hi, I'm Graham Nash," the first guy said, sticking out his hand.

No way.

Graham Nash, rhythm guitarist for the Hollies, the guy who sang the high parts in all those groovy-smooth harmonies. And Bernie Calvert was with him, their bass player. I'd just bought the *Hollies Greatest Hits* album right after Christmas. "Look through Any Window," "I Can't Let Go," "Bus Stop," "Pay You Back with Interest," "On a Carousel," "Carrie Anne"—I couldn't get enough of Nash's voice.

"Dean Kohler," I said, shaking Nash's hand. I couldn't believe I was standing there with Graham Nash. Calvert gave me a nod, then wandered off.

Nash pointed to the equipment. "You know how to operate all of these things?" he asked, bewildered.

I nodded. "I'm also a musician."

Nash looked interested. "Oh, yeah? What instrument?"

"Guitar."

Nash looked really interested. "Acoustic or electric?"

"Both."

"Yeah, me too," he said, like he was just some guy who dabbled with guitar in his spare time. He leaned back on my desk, making himself comfortable, crossing one leg over the other. "I used to play just acoustic, but now . . ."

We talked for a long time. About Gibsons. About Gretsches. About how popular Vox amplifiers were, how all of the American bands wanted Vox amps because the English bands used them.

"Funny thing," Nash said, "we English blokes would prefer Fender amps. But they're tough as the dickens to bring over and cost a pretty penny as well. Now a lot of the English bands are using Marshall amps."

It was like talking to an old friend. He was just a regular guy. No rock-star ego. And he was chatting with me like I was a fellow musician. An equal. It seemed like the most natural thing in the world.

I offered him a Coke from the machine in the hall. After a while, our conversation turned to the road.

"How do you like touring the U.S.?" I asked.

"It's brilliant, really, we like it a lot," he said. "We've met a lot of great people, seen a lot of new places. We're lucky enough to have big records in America and in Europe, so the tours have been successful in both."

The way he said it, I took "successful" to mean "money-making." As in income-producing.

As in a job.

A real job.

A real good job.

We talked some more, about songwriting, recording. I could have talked all night.

"You know," he said, draining the last of his soda, "the secret in the music business is to record, record, and record some more. Before anyone can see that you're a success, they have to hear it first."

A page from the control room interrupted us. The director wanted the Hollies in the studio.

"They're ready for you," I said. We rounded up Calvert and headed over to the cameras.

The Hollies taped a lip-synched version of "Jennifer Eccles," from their *Evolution* album. I'd been working on that one at home with my buddies. The Hollies were so pro, they nailed it in one take.

I watched from behind the videotape machine.

And for the first time since I'd been back home, I knew exactly what I was supposed to do.

The next day I called Roy.

"I want to make a record. . . ."

Epilogue

With Roy's help, I did make another record, a 45 rpm single of two of my own songs, the Jimi Hendrix–influenced "Gooseberry Pie" and an updated version of "The Next Boy," from the old Satellites demo. Three friends backed me on the session: George Newsome, a former next-door neighbor, on bass; Robert Craig on keyboards; and Johnny Johnston on drums. I used my remaining Banana bucks to pay for the studio time.

When my cousin Cecil returned from the army, I formed another band, the Soft Light, with Cecil on bass, Lynde Gillam, also of the Satellites, on drums, and Robert Craig. The following TV season, with a different drummer, *we* became the house band on WAVY's *Disc-O-Ten* program.

The next two years were difficult. Cecil, close as a brother and my bass player since day one, was killed in a car crash.

There was a revolving door of musicians joining and leaving my band. But I was a working musician, a professional musician, performing on television and in clubs, making a living from my music.

I was following my dream.

Though I'm not sure if my father respected my decision, he did come to accept it. Not long after I formed the Soft Light, I basically took over Dad's garage. I covered the walls, ceiling, and door with thick packing quilts, transforming it into the perfect soundproof rehearsal room. Dad's Catalina and my GTO had to live outside. Dad never complained; he never said a word. In fact, he soon replaced one of my bedroom windows at the back corner of the house with a door so I could load my gear in and out of my room in the wee hours of the morning without waking everyone up banging the stuff down the hallway. It was his idea, and he did all the work himself.

In the seventies, my best and longest-running group, Mad Wax, lasted the entire decade. In the eighties and nineties, I had a successful tribute band that played material from the fifties and sixties, including many of the songs I wrote and performed in the Satellites and the Banana.

I have remained in the music business to this day. Now I run my own media promotion and advertising company that provides sound and video production.

Over the decades, I've played with dozens of musicians, in many bands, under a variety of circumstances. But the best band camaraderie I've ever known was with a group of guys known as the Electrical Banana.

Captain Leadbetter's unswerving confidence in me was the starting point. He didn't ask me if it was possible to form a band or if I thought I could do it. He *told* me to do it, with no doubt in his mind that the band would become a reality.

From virtually nothing, we evolved into one smooth-running unit. And not because of me, but because of Mike Ioli, Jon Sugden, and Ben Jessen. I already knew how to make a band work; they had to start from scratch.

And they never wavered.

They made the Electrical Banana happen . . . and they helped me through the most difficult year of my life. What I valued most was deep inside me. Music. With their help, during a time when none of us knew for sure if we would live or die, I came to know the true power of music—to communicate, heal, connect. Unite.

For this I am forever grateful to Jon, Mike, and Ben. I will never forget them.